PARADISE

First published in Great Britain, the USA and
Canada in 2020 by Canongate Books Ltd,
14 High Street, Edinburgh EH1 1TE

Distributed in the USA by Publishers Group West
and in Canada by Publishers Group Canada

canongate.co.uk

1

The author gratefully acknowledges the
support of Creative Scotland towards
the publication of this book

British Library Cataloguing-in-Publication Data
A catalogue record for this book is available
on request from the British Library

ISBN 978 1 78689 474 8

Typeset in Times New Roman 13/14 pt
by Palimpsest Book Production Ltd,
Falkirk, Stirlingshire

Printed and bound in Great Britain
by Clays Ltd, Elcograf S.p.A.

MIX
Paper from
responsible sources
FSC
www.fsc.org   FSC® C018072

PARADISE

DANTE'S DIVINE TRILOGY PART 3
ENGLISHED IN PROSAIC VERSE
BY
ALASDAIR GRAY

CANONGATE BOOKS
EDINBURGH 2020

CANTOS

1: The First Ascent

1   God's glory moves and shows the universe
shining in some parts more, in others less.
I entered Heaven with joy too great for speech

4   to glorify his light. I can recall
only dim shadows of it now
within this song. All you nine muses

7   led by Virgil helped me evoke the steep
descent to Hell and climb to reach this height.
Sun-king Apollo too inspired their aid!

10 I beg you, please give me such strength again,
turn me into a perfect voice to sing
of Heaven's grandest things and crown myself

13 with laurels, the one headgear fit for use
by a true poet or great conqueror.
Their fewness demonstrates in human kind

16 a shameful lack of will. If I succeed,
like spark from which flames leap, some after me
may be inspired to write with greater skill.

19 The sunrise greets us most days of the year
from several degrees to north or south.
When solar orbit touches other rings

(equators earthly and celestial,   22
ecliptic and the equinoctial)
four circles make three crosses and so bring

more harmony, and Summer can begin.   25
The sun this morning rose at that good point.
When Beatrice looked up at height of noon

no eagle ever fixed upon the sun   28
a gaze as clear, and since reflected rays
rebound to source like pilgrims going home,

twin beams of light now linked her sight and sun.   31
I copied her. Eden was made for ease
of humankind. There it was possible

for me to see what here would make me blind.   34
Gazing into the solar blaze I saw,
like molten silver splashed from crucible,

such fountains of tremendous light I thought   37
that He Who Can had made an extra sun.
I saw too Beatrice now looked upon

the high, eternal, starry, singing wheels   40
so lowering my eyes to rest on hers
I heard them too. Eating a magic herb

changed Glaucus to an ancient Greek sea-god.   43
The love-light in the face of Beatrice
transhumaned me in ways I cannot say.

Of new sensations knowledge cannot speak   46
unless it learns new words. Did God lift up
my eager mind to his eternal sphere?

49 No rain or river filled so vast a lake
as this whole sky now kindled into flame.
The brilliance of its harmony and light

52 provoked an appetite to know the cause,
so she who understood me perfectly
smiling replied before I questioned her,

55 "Dullard, do you not see you've left the earth?
Lightning never flashed faster from a cloud
than we ascend to your right place and mine."

58 Her smile and words erased perplexities
before I found one more. "But why," said I,
"does solid me rise above lighter things?"

61 Like mother soothing sickly child she said,
"Order is God's first law. All that He made
have places in eternal excellence, for which

64 in minerals, plants, animals they strive
instinctively, in people willingly.
When ill will leads astray our souls can't rest

67 until we reach our given place and are
at last in harmony with all that's best.
We are now soaring to our origin

70 as naturally as a waterfall
pours down a cliff. Those who forget their place
by choosing base delight, are very like

73 materials no artist can use well,
discarded in the midden heaps of Hell.
Climbing them there has purified you, so

guilt cannot weight you. That is why you rise.   76
Innocent souls who stay below defy
nature and reason, like a static flame."

Pausing, she turned her eyes toward the sky.   79

2: Moon Sphere

1 Some folk in little boats follow my ship
because they like the story in my song.
Let them turn back toward the shore they know

4 unless their craft is strong. I now go far
over a sea no poet crossed before.
Minerva fills my sails. Apollo steers.

7 The Muses indicate each guiding star.
If you are of the few like me who seek
the bread that feeds but never satisfies,

10 you too may launch your vessel on this sea
using my wake as guide. The Argonauts,
those heroes voyaging for the Golden Fleece,

13 when they saw armed men springing from the soil
after their captain ploughed down dragon teeth
were not as much amazed as you will be.

16 Our inborn thirst for God's sufficiency
kept Beatrice intent on upper skies,
me intent on her eyes, so up we went

19 as swiftly as we looked, until halted
by a wondrous sight. It stopped us short
as a struck target ends an arrow flight.

"Now praise God for His generosity!   22
This star is nearest earth," said happily
that fairest one who understood my mind.

I saw what lower down could not exist.   25
Luminous mist enclosed us now inside
a diamond-hard and perfect shining pearl,

yet we could move in it as easily   28
as light rays pass through water in a glass
without a change of character in each.

For one or more bodies to occupy   31
an equally dense body easily
defies earth's common sense. In Paradise

it was quite clear to my intelligence.   34
"Lady," said I, "my gratitude to He
who saves us from death's grip will never cease,

but why, when viewed from where most people live, 37
has this pure moon a spotted face? Some say
they can make out Cain and his thornbush there."

Amused she said, "Wits stray when seeking laws   40
for what they cannot touch, so tell me now
what you think the cause." "Varied density?"

I suggested. "Looking through dirty air?"   43
"No," said she. "God has made all the Heavens
equally good. Air here is free from dirt,

and though bodies of light within these skies   46
differ in sizes, colours, faculties,
their densities do not. On summer days

49 most things appear equally clear at noon.
   At night when you see bodies in one sphere
   what you mistake for spots .are smaller lights

52 contrasted with more bright, as in the moon."

3: In the Moon

She who, sunlike, first warmed my breast with love   1
deserved both gratitude for that reply
and for correcting me. Raising my eyes,

surprise expelled my thanks. I thought she stood   4
beside a dusty glass that mirrored folk
so faintly that a pearl on a pale brow

was not more dim. They seemed to beckon me.   7
Narcissus loved reflections of himself
so gazed in front. To see these folk more clear

I looked behind myself, and none were there.   10
Turning again to my sweet smiling guide
I heard her say, "Funny, the childish way

you do not trust your eyes in Paradise!   13
These beings by my side are real although
lowest in Heaven for breaking holy vows.

Question them. Hear. Believe. They shine in truth   16
and never more will truth depart from them."
I faced the shade that seemed most keen to speak

and almost stammering with eagerness   19
declared, "O spirit made for blessedness,
who dwells in sweetness of this radiance,

22 will you be kind enough to let me know
your name and circumstance?" She eagerly
and cheerfully told me, "We can't refuse

25 kindness to those who only want what's right
because at our great height above the earth
all are like God in this. On earth I was

28 your friend Forese's sister, Piccarda,
forced to wed someone who I did not love.
Soon after I was dead. My fairer face

31 is why you do not recognise me now."
"Piccarda! Yes, I know you," I declared,
"although at first the glory in your face

34 half-blinded, dazed, distracted me. But say,
is not a higher sphere what you desire?
In higher places you'd be held more dear."

37 She smiled a bit (as did the other shades)
then answered me so gladly that she seemed
in the first fires of love. "Brother, our wills

40 are tuned by charity – by love itself.
We thirst for what we have, and nothing more.
Our wills are now identical with His

43 who keeps all things in perfect harmony –
earth, planets, stars, up to the outermost
circumference of all, which is Himself.

46 Any in Paradise who craved for more
(and once before this craving did occur)
would strike a discord through our bliss and sever

charity from necessity, and thus   49
destroy the harmony of Heaven too.
God's will is the creative sea in which

we live and move. Sharing it is our peace."   52
I now knew why the bliss of Paradise
is everywhere in Heaven – each soul

is needed by the whole domain, although   55
God is not always equally in all.
Yet in my body my imperfect will

still craved more water from her well of truth.   58
The pure cloth of the life she'd tried to weave
was slashed before the fabric was complete.

I begged Piccarda to explain. Said she,   61
"A perfect love of Christ allowed Saint Clare
to teach the vows by which a lady may

put on the bridal veil and marry Him.   64
Just such a nun was I who left the world
to join the Poor Clare sisterhood. Alas,

greedy relations came, dragged me away.   67
God knew my sufferings. Upon my right,
shining with all the splendour of the moon

is one whose plight was mine. Raped from cloister,   70
keeping bridal veil over her heart, she
is Constance, heiress to the Swabian throne,

mother of Europe's holy potentate   73
who should have been the Roman Emperor."
Piccarda, singing *Ave Maria*,

76 sank from my eyes into deeper light like
stone in pond. I looked to Beatrice who
increased so vividly upon my sight,

79 questioning her was more than I could do.

4: More Moonlight

Between two equally enticing meals 1
an idiot might starve before he chose.
A lamb between two wolves would also doubt

which way to turn, or hound between two does. 4
I hungered after what my guide might say
if asked why Heaven's justice seemed unkind,

but can a man God made doubt God is good? 7
I feared to ask that question choking me,
but Beatrice, who understood my mind

replied at once, "What ties your tongue is this: 10
how can good vows and wills deserve the less
if broken by another's wickedness?

Your other doubt is astrological. 13
Plato wrote after death all souls return
to planets ruling them. Did moons decree

these nuns' inconstancy? Both these doubts need 16
an answer. I will take the second first.
It is most poisonous, so listen hard.

No seraphim that is most one with God – 19
not Abraham, Moses or Samuel –
neither John Baptist or Evangelist –

22 not even Mary in the highest Heaven
is separated from the two you've met
although they chose to greet you in this sphere.

25 All share alike in the eternal bliss
according to their soul's capacity.
To indicate the nature of life here

28 I am compelled to talk to you as if
Heavenly Paradise has social ranks
like those on earth. This is not so, but I

31 can only make the highest things more clear
by speaking of them in the words you know,
although they may mislead. God's Scriptures say

34 He sees, acts, speaks with eyes, hands, mouth because
only thus men and women can conceive
One seeing with all light, whose deeds are days,

37 whose voices teach in all that can be heard:
thunder and waves, birdsong and whispered speech.
Plato says after death all souls return

40 to stars they left at birth, meaning perhaps
natural forces shape our characters
to some extent. If so this partial truth

43 has misled worshippers of sun and moon,
Venus and Mars, who treat these stars as gods.
Your other doubt can do no mischief here

46 or lose the smallest droplet of my love.
That in your eyes justice seems cruelty
is not a sign of heresy, but faith.

By all who know that Jesus Christ is God,   49
doubts can be logically overcome.
Doubt should make faith more sure. The facts are these.

No force can make a flame burn upside down   52
or alter any wholly pure good will,
though force may twist them sideways or depress.

To show that torture could not change his mind   55
Saint Lawrence chose to roast upon a grill
and Mucius compelled his hand to burn.

Rare are heroic virtues of that kind.   58
When stronger forces make good nuns break vows
and leave their cloisters, they are not to blame,

yet must feel shame if the strong force withdraws 61
and she does not return because the rape
has cracked her spirit, left her in the wrong.

If that is understood your doubts are solved.   64
Here is a greater doubt you can't resolve
without my aid. I told you Piccarda

is at the source of truth, so cannot lie.   67
She said that Constance, forced to be a queen
and breed an emperor, stayed nun at heart.

This means she did not linger in the wrong   70
by choosing to conform with what was forced.
Why was this so? Some sin against their will,

thinking to save themselves from something worse. 73
Alcmaeon slew his mother to escape
his father's curse. Perverse good will enforced

76 is a Hell brew, but brother, know Constance
   suffered by violence, but she forced none.
   Only goodness came from her suffering,

79 so absolute Good Will took no offence
   but the reverse, as Piccarda told you,
   and also in these other words do I."

82 Such were the ripples of that holy stream
   whose source was the clear fountain of all truth.
   They quenched and satisfied my thirsty soul.

85 I told her, "You who the First Lover loves,
   whose speech raises my thinking nearer His
   I now see intellects can never rest

88 until at last the One Truth shines on them
   and further truth beyond cannot exist.
   Doubt is a sturdy tree rooted in truth.

91 Nature demands we fly from branch to branch,
   from height to height up to the topmost twig.
   Only when that is reached can active mind

94 rest like contented bird inside its nest.
   Were that not so then all desire is vain.
   Lady, these facts lead to a new request.

97 Could all who fail to act as they have vowed
   provide what God requires? Redeem themselves
   through other acts of generosity?"

100 The eyes of Beatrice now sparkled bright
    with the new interest that lifted me
    so far above normality that I

103 could hardly bear the sight of so much love.

5: Free Will and Mercury

"Don't wonder that in loving warmth I shine 1
more vividly than mortal eyes can bear.
The light of truth now growing in your mind

mirrors the highest good and so is bound 4
to kindle greater love in me, though since
you loved me as a child you've been beguiled

by many gleams of truth in lesser things. 7
You ask me now if souls can be redeemed
by good works when they break a holy vow."

Having begun this chapter with the words 10
of Beatrice, here follows her reply,
her answer to the things I wished to know:

"The greatest gift God gave when He made men 13
was what is greatest glory in Himself:
free will, a function of intelligence.

Only humanity possesses that. 16
We are the only beasts who worship Him
with rights of sacrifice, with priests and nuns

who promise they will do God's will alone 19
by sacrificing all their will to Him.
A given sacrifice that's taken back

22 is ill-got gain, like any other gift
lawlessly repossessed. Can thieves use well
what they have stolen? They are robbers still.

25 Remember that chief point. Though Holy Church
sometimes releases priests and nuns from vows
which seems to contradict the truth I've told,

28 regard that as a mouthful of tough meat
to carefully chew over as I speak.
Think hard and you will come to understand

31 a sacrifice has two parts. There is first
promise of gift, and then the given thing.
A promise is not cancelled if not kept.

34 Only the keeping of one wipes it out,
but Jewish law said promises stayed good
if witnesses and parties to the deed

37 agreed upon a substituted gift
of greater value than the promised one.
Our church accepts this law of substitute,

40 but lets no single person use that law
till a just judge, weighing with equal scales,
can demonstrate no fraud or force prevails.

43 We Christians should be slow to swear an oath
and having sworn should strive to keep our word,
but not like Jephtha, Agamemnon too,

46 who slaughtered daughters rather than revoke
the hasty, cruel vows that proved them fools.
O Christians, learn to be a steadier folk.

We have both Testaments, the Old and New,
and further guidance, for our Holy Church
has shepherds known to every one of you.

These should be all we need to save our souls.
Don't leave your mothers' milk like silly lambs
who think the world is made for fretful play.

Do not be led astray by wicked greed
so any Jew who keeps his rabbi's laws
can point to you in scornful mockery."

I write these words as Beatrice spoke them
before she looked up longingly to where
the universe was sending down most light.

Her silence and her ardent face imposed
a quietness upon my eager will
as, like an arrow striking the bull's eye

before the string impelling it is still,
we sped up to the second sphere, and here
her bliss increased and Heaven brightened too.

What did this greater brightness do to me
who am so liable to change? New bliss
left me no words to say more than I saw.

As in a calm clear pool the fishes come
expecting food from one upon the rim
I saw a thousand splendours drawing near

and heard from each, "Here's one who brings more love!"
As these souls neared us they appeared more full,
more radiant with shining happiness.

76 Dear reader, if my story ended here,
how eagerly you'd want to know the rest.
I say so to make plain how much I wished

79 to hear about the state these souls possessed.
This happened when a voice addressed me straight.
"O you who, born for virtue, travel here

82 before the warfare of your life is done,
since it is given you to view the thrones
which the eternally triumphant won,

85 ask what you wish and I will answer you."
"Ask anything you want," Beatrice cried,
"and trust the answers as if gods replied."

88 The speaker nestled finely in a glow
that shone from his serenely smiling eyes.
I thanked him for his courtesy then said,

91 "Please tell me of yourself and Mercury,
smallest of spheres between the moon and sun,
planet least known because the rays least strong."

94 Then, like the sun seen through dissolving mist
joy made him brighten till excess of light
prevented seeing him. I heard his words

97 which sound in the next chapter of my song.

6: Justinian

"Three hundred years after the birth of Christ   1
Constantine led the Roman Eagle east
near ruined Troy from which Aeneas fled

and built its nest on Europe's farthest coast.   4
This new Rome was the Empire's capital
while old Rome stayed the home of Papacy.

When Goths invading Italy destroyed   7
Rome's earthly strength, they did not harm the Pope.
That was before I wore the Empire's crown

and hailed as Caesar – am Justinian.   10
God's love led me to unify Rome's laws
into one useful code, weeding out words

that might pervert the justice of a cause.   13
I was unfit for this great task at first.
My faith was still impure, for I believed

Christ was the Holy Ghost in manlike shape,   16
not flesh and blood. A letter from the Pope
corrected me, then Heaven gave me peace.

Count Belisarius, my general,   19
drove Goths from Italy, and so again
around Earth's Middle Sea one emperor

22 ruled all, and there my legal code was used,
and thus Rome's Empire worked at giving birth
to what Augustine said all should create:

25 God's Citadel on Earth. My peaceful rule
made Church and State supreme yet separate.
You know me now, but I have more to tell

28 of how the Roman Empire got renown
and used it well centuries after me
before the Whigs and Tories broke it down.

31 Aeneas toiled for years on lands and seas
before his wedding to a Latin queen
gave a new home to Trojan refugees,

34 the ancestors of Rome. For centuries
their fighting royalty, wise senators
conquered kingdoms and communes. Rome's Eagle

37 flew through Europe, Africa, Asia,
forcing far-flung nations into one vaster,
longer-lasting state than in his brief life

40 the great Alexander could create.
The time arrived when Heaven wanted peace.
The Roman Eagle perched on Caesar's fist,

43 none being fit to manage it but he.
No tongue, no pen does justice to his deeds,
quelling revolting principalities,

46 crossing the Rubicon, then putting down
the civil war in Gaul, Spain, Egypt, Greece.
Satan in Hell chews those who murdered him.

There Cleopatra weeps. She chose to die   49
by snakebite to escape the Eagle's beak.
Augustus Caesar was its master next.

He spread the Empire to the Red Sea shore,   52
declared the *Pax Romana* everywhere,
and needed to support it by a tax,

so ordered men back to their place of birth   55
for registration. Thus in Bethlehem
our Prince of Peace was born. Now listen hard!

Tiberius was Caesar number three.   58
Under his reign the Eagle did one thing
upon a hill outside Jerusalem

that makes all other splendid Roman deeds   61
look small and dim when viewed by Christian eyes.
Here God's wrath made the Eagle work for Him —

helped God Himself revenge Himself on God.   64
Later, when Titus reigned, Heaven ensured
vengeance on that revenge for ancient sin.

The Roman legions slew Hebrew hordes,   67
looted and burned Solomon's synagogue,
made a whole ruin of Jerusalem.

Look forward now. When Whiggish Lombard crows 70
tried to peck out Pope Leo's tongue, he found
protection in Emperor Charlemagne.

Rome's bishop and Imperial Eagle then   73
were allies though apart, as they should be.
Look at the state of politics today!

76 Now ancient symbols of the common good
   achieved by men whose fame is like my own
   are used on flag and badge to foster hate

79 by greedy statesmen with short local aims.
   The Roman Eagle and the Fleur de Lys
   are trampled by a squabbling multitude.

82 We in this little star strove to do well,
   but also strove for fame, so rose less far
   than those whose virtues lacked all selfishness.

85 This we cannot regret, happy to know
   good choirs all sound the more melodious
   where diverse voices sing both high and low.

88 In this pearl also shines the light of one
   not quite as grand as mighty emperors.
   He worked as hard for goodness as did we

91 but won no great reward. His birth was low
   and name was Romeo, and he became
   an honest steward of Count Berenger –

94 served him so well, four daughters of the Count
   got such rich dowries that they married kings.
   Envy declared he filled his pockets too,

97 which was untrue. Dismissed, he had to beg.
   Though he is famous, those who honour him
   would do it much more if they understood,

100 how sore it is to beg your livelihood."

7: Beatrice Explains

"To Heaven's greatest height now praise our God 1
who gloriously brightens with His rays
good hearth-fires everywhere on holy days!"

So sang that bright soul, dancing as he sang, 4
that ruler who had striven to connect
justice on earth and Heaven's government.

In happy play the other shining souls 7
danced with him too, until like shooting stars
they disappeared by being far away

and left me brooding in perplexity. 10
I well knew Beatrice could quell my doubts
so *Tell her! Tell her!* sounded in my head,

but reverence had overcome my tongue. 13
Parts of her name (*be, is*) still strike me dumb.
She did not leave me thus, for with a smile

that would have cheered a burning man she said, 16
"You do not see why justice should demand
vengeance upon revenge for ancient sin?

Listen and hear true doctrine straight from me. 19
Adam, the only man not born but made,
was given all good things men can enjoy

22 but could not bear one curb upon his will
so damned himself and we who spring from him.
Long ages passed before the Word of God

25 descending worked to free us from this ill.
By one act of amazing love God took
body with we who have rejected Him,

28 became a sinner too, deserving death
like me and you, and in Gethsemane
sadly embraced that foul necessity,

31 accepting Roman law so none can say
our Maker never felt our suffering.
If human need for death is understood

34 indeed Christ's death was good. If we respect
His righteousness, nothing was more unjust.
From that great act came opposite effects –

37 Christ's death desired by God *and* Jewish priests,
for which earth quaked and Heaven opened wide,
and Solomon's great temple was destroyed.

40 I fear your thoughts are fankled in a knot
you can't untie. Although my words are clear,
why God redeemed us thus is dark to you.

43 Brother, it is dark to everyone
with minds unripened by the sun of love.
I'll say it all again in other words.

46 God's excellence is never envious,
so all the souls He makes possess like Him
eternal life; like Him, freedom of choice.

These gifts are lost by people choosing sin.   49
Adam and Eve disobeyed God; believed
rejecting God would make them equal Him,

thus they exchanged eternity for time.   52
Justice cannot ignore so bad a crime
which all folk born of women re-enact,

so gaps between ourselves and Paradise   55
are far too big for penitence to fill
by any single act of human will

though penitence is certainly required.   58
Only a miracle could reconcile
justice with mercy, and at last it came.

God's overflowing goodness made His Word   61
human, like us; offered new birth, new life,
eternally to all who follow Christ

and grasp their cross – forgive who do them wrong –   64
love enemies and promise not to sin.
What better thing to save us could God do

than show all people how we ought to live?   67
I see you want more news of sacred things,
a thirst I'll satisfy before you ask.

What troubles you is instability.   70
God made the earth and water, fire and air
so must have made them pure as Paradise –

pure as these starry spheres, this shining space   73
through which we rise. Why on earth do all things
change, age, sicken, die and rot? Here is why.

76 Our God Himself did not directly make
all of the world below. Live plants and beasts
are generated in His elements

79 by things He made before. Sunlight is one.
Yet on the sixth day of the Genesis
He breathed His own soul into human clay.

82 All other earthly life will suffer death.
Men, women are the great exception,
created by His love to love Him back

85 eternally, after resurrection."

8: Venus

Pagans have wrongly thought the brightest star 1
at dawn and dusk provoked the wildest love.
Venus was offered hymns and sacrifice

as lover of Mars, playboy Cupid's mother, 4
provider of erotic joy beside
sorrow that drove Dido to suicide.

I only knew we'd soared up to love's sphere 7
on seeing Beatrice grew lovelier.
Bright dancing lights were in that shining globe

like sparks in a flame, like many voices 10
harmonised in one great organ tone.
The lights spun fast and slow like seraphim

according to (I think) their view of God 13
until, aware of us, a stream of them
unwound and, comet-like, sped to our side

singing a welcoming *hosanna*. How 16
I wished and always wish to hear that sound!
The first light said, "May we share happiness?

Instruct us, poet, how to please you best. 19
On earth you wrote of how our intellects
move the third star. We love you much for that.

22 Pausing, conversing now with you will be
a very blissful interval of rest."
I looked to my bright guide to find if she

25 accepted this, received her smiling nod,
so asked, "Please, who are you?" – not words that said
how glad I was, and yet he knew because

28 I saw his glow increase as he replied,
"If dazzling joy did not disguise my form
like smooth cocoon protecting a silk worm

31 you would see Charles Martel, a long-gone friend
who dwelled too short a time on earth to stop
the Whigs and Tories rending Italy.

34 O Florentine, had plague not ended me
(king of Naples, Sicily, Hungary,
count of Provence) you would not be exiled.

37 My father's second son is Naples' king
and has not learned the art of ruling men,
for brother Robert does not even know

40 taxing the poor too much must breed revolt.
One of our blood who did not heed that fact
incited massacre in Palermo –

43 mobs filling streets and yelling *kill kill kill!*
Unlike our dad, Robert alas is mean,
grabs wealth through knights who share his greed for gold.

46 He won't get rid of them, although the cost
of keeping them wrecks all good government."
"Sir Charles," said I, "the Heaven-sent joy you bring

is also yours who, now so near to God, 49
knows from Whom purest loving wisdom flows.
You've made me glad, so now please make me wise.

How can good seed grow into rotten fruit? 52
Why is bad son bred from a decent dad?"
"If you can grasp the truth of my reply,"

said he, "you will understand many things 55
upon which you have so far turned your back:
what moves and satisfies this Paradise

you now ascend, gives planets influence 58
over those born below. Each embryo
receives a starry ray, like shaft from bow,

that shapes its character. 61
No soul is quite alike, yet can combine
in godly ways with other souls on earth,

just as the planets circulate above. 64
Were this not so the universe would be
a chaos too confused to form a star

or any form of life, but all we see 67
amounts to one tremendous work of art.
Even its smallest part has unity

through balanced interchange of energy. 70
Is that quite clear?" I said, "Yes, I agree.
Nature has made the world just what we see."

"Can men live well without societies?" 73
asked he. I said, "One perhaps sometimes may,
but not for long. None could begin to live

76 without a family." He answered, "Right.
A family is a society,
but think as citizen. Cities require

79 all kinds of skill: nurses for babies and
farmers for food, builders, tradesmen, doctors
for the ill, engineers like Daedalus

82 law-givers like Solon, artists like Phidias,
priests like Melchizedek and commanders
like Xerxes. Cities can exist because

85 star influence insists that lads are *not*
exact copies of their dads. That is why
pagans believed gods fathered their heroes.

88 Bastard Romulus was called son of Mars.
Brothers (as well I know) can differ too
even when twins, as Esau and Jacob show.

91 I love you, so will tell you something more.
When by bad luck people are doing work
unsuited to their nature, things go wrong

94 and a good land has chosen the wrong way
when fighters preach in time of peace, and then
in time of war the loud-mouthed clergymen

97 climb up to seize the general command."

9: Prophecies

Mother or wife of Charles, if you read this,   1
know that he spoke of woe ahead for you
and his posterity, but also said,

"Don't speak of it. Let the years take their course.   4
Tell them that Paradise will note their tears,
and justice crush who causes them. That's sure."

He, loving holy light, now faced the sun   7
whose goodness is the main wealth we require.
Alas, for foolish creatures who admire

only the works of human vanity.   10
Another shining soul approaching me,
revealed delight by its increasing glow.

Beatrice once more signalling assent   13
I cried out, "Bless'd spirit, please let me know
what you have come to make me understand."

The light whose face I could not see replied,   16
"In the degraded land of Italy,
between the isles of Venice and the springs

from which the Brenta and Piave flow,   19
is the Romano stronghold, whose tough lord
with fire and sword plunders the plain below.

22 He was my brother Ezzelino, who
is boiling now with other brutal men
in Hell's hot river of the blood they shed.

25 I am Cunizza, widely known because
so often conquered by this brilliant star.
Venus helped me inspire a troubadour

28 and follow where he led. Though often wed
I always could forgive myself, although
good citizens like you will find that strange.

31 The poet you see gleaming at my side
has written what ensures his lasting fame.
In our first life we all should do so well

34 that people later smile to hear our name,
but who thinks so in Padua where mobs
now dominate that unrepenting state?

37 Defeated once, destruction comes again
and the day nears when Paduan blood will stain
boggy Vicenza's mud. In Travigi one lord

40 still holding his head high will die
by assassin's hand. Feltro will bewail
her bishop who breaks sanctuary vows

43 giving to slaughter those he should protect.
No fouler priest was ever clapped in jail.
The barrels must be big if they'll contain

46 gore of Farrarese slain by courtesy
of that vile cleric's proof he is a Whig.
Such vileness suits his city's evil ways.

Angelic mirrors up in Heaven's height   49
(you call them thrones) reflect God's judgement down
to we who have the right to say such things."

Here she returned to dancing in her sphere,   52
leaving the other spirit at my side.
Like a rare jewel caught in ray of light

he now was sparkling with a ruby glow,   55
for in that place a greater brightness comes
with gladness, just as laughter happens here,

and darkness deepens grievous gloom in Hell.   58
Said I, "The seraphim robed in six wings
well know what God perceives, and so do you.

Were I in you as you exist in me,   61
I'd not delay in saying what you will."
Said he, "The vastest valley in the world

flooded by ocean, is the Middle Sea.   64
My birthplace on its shore was Genoa
where the third planet's ray moulded my clay.

Called Folco, I was bishop of Marseilles   67
after my hair turned grey, but earlier
I doubt if Hercules, Phyllis, Dido,

were more amorous. I do not rejoice   70
in having sinned. Forgiveness blesses us
so happily, we know and share the love

moving our Heaven above the earth below.   73
Please listen more before ascending more.
This brightness like a sunbeam at my side

76 gleaming in clearest water, was the whore
Rahab, one of Christ's ancestors
freed from death by His Resurrection

79 with Adam, Eve, Abraham and the rest.
Jesus made Rahab foremost in this sphere
(last planet touched by shadow of the earth)

82 for she helped Joshua to victory
when taking Palestine, that holy land
God gave his chosen folk, land conquered since

85 by Saracens, whom modern popes ignore.
O Florentine, a founder of your state
worshipped the first sworn enemy of God!

88 There grow the golden florins, currency
of worldwide trade and worldwide jealousy.
That gold has led astray both sheep and lambs

91 by turning shepherds into hungry beasts.
The Words of God and theologians
are studied less by popes and cardinals

94 than books of canon law telling how fines,
penalties and wills can accumulate
property for priests. They think less about

97 Nazareth where Gabriel spread his wings
announcing Christ will come, than about Rome
where Peter and many who followed him

100 came to be crucified; think more about
the Vatican's bank vaults than saving souls.
Why will Church and Nation not win free of

103 wealth's despicable adulteration?

10: The Sun

The Father, Son and Holy Ghost unite   1
to nourish worlds below in time and space
with flow of endless love and endless light.

Raise your eyes with me, reader, to the skies!   4
Who recognise the glory there, taste God,
giver of warmth even the blind can feel

combining bodies in the universe.   7
Each part of it shows the Creator's art
keeping the movement neat. A fool may think

the cosmos squint. No planet goes agley.   10
If planets strayed a fraction more or less
out of their orbits, crashes would ensue.

Reader, stay with this book. Because you glimpse   13
the daring of its scope before the end
you may feel weariness, yet find delight.

Now comes the food I cannot make you eat.   16
Here I describe experience beyond
reach of both common sense and common speech.

Beatrice raised me to each higher state   19
so softly, instantly, it took no time.
I did not notice how I came to be

22 within the sun, that ministry of light
revealing breadth of space and time of day.
The people in the sun were all so bright

25 I saw them clearly through its radiance
which is our source of light. How this could be
I cannot say. Believe me, it was true.

28 Said Beatrice, "Praises and thanks are due
the Son of God who lifted you into
this sun of Paradise." No mortal heart,

31 I think, loved Jesus more than I did then,
in adoration quite forgetting she
who laughed aloud with joy to see me thus.

34 And then I saw a ring of shining souls
surrounding us like halo round the moon.
Only the sweetness of their tongues excelled

37 the glory of their smiling eyes, a sound
more wonderful than words can tell. Take wings –
fly to the solar sphere to hear that song.

40 The splendours circled us like stars around
the Arctic pole three times, and then they paused
like dancers waiting for another tune.

43 Before it came I heard a near one say,
"Your thirst for knowledge glows within your face.
I cannot keep it from you any more

46 than clouds can keep their showers from the sea.
You wish to know the flowers in this wreath
garlanding lovingly the fair one who

strengthens you here. Know that I was a lamb   49
of that well-ordered flock Dominic led,
where is good fattening, unless we stray.

That great instructor Albert of Cologne   52
is on my right. He taught me how to see
Greek science strengthens Christ's theology.

I am Thomas Aquinas. Let my words   55
lead your eyes round this circle of the bless'd
and introduce the rest. Gratian is next

who reconciled the laws of Church and State;   58
then modest scholar Peter Abelard,
wise commentator on prophetic lore.

See the fifth light, most beautiful of all!   61
Solomon he, whose wisdom was so great
none ever rose as high; then Dionysius,

teacher of angelic hierarchies.   64
Orosius, the small light after him,
taught Christian history to Augustine.

My praises now have led you through seven lights.   67
The next is excellent Boethius
whose writing shows the world's deceits, and how

we all can gain peace here through martyrdom.   70
See flaming after him four lights of God:
encyclopaedic Isadore; and Bede

the venerable English monk; Richard   73
the mystic Scot; and then before your eyes
return to me, see one from whose grave thoughts

76 came truths some did not want to know – Siger!"
That twelfth name sounded like a striking clock
telling the time when a whole Church must rise

79 to sing the praise of Jesus Christ our King.
Now half the solar voices drew or drove
the rest to chime in harmony so sweet

82 my spirits soared to join the melody
as the glad golden sun-sphere carried round
that choir, adding such glory to word

85 only in endless joy can they be heard.

11: Of Francis

O daft deliriums of earthbound men!   1
With force or fraud you fight to gather wealth
by trade or law, priest-craft or shedding blood,

then glut your appetites on luxuries,   4
corrupting sense by wasteful indolence,
driving your mental wings into foul mud.

Freed from such emptiness by Beatrice   7
I stood a guest among the bless'd who danced
around us like a splendid galaxy.

Then pausing as before, that radiance   10
who first had spoken spoke to me again,
smiling and glowing brighter as he did.

"Because all here share in the mind of God   13
I see some words of mine engendered doubt:
there is good fattening unless we stray;

as also these: *none ever rose so high.*   16
To clarify I'll speak at greater length.
The Providence that rules the world of men

cannot be absolutely understood   19
by human minds. To wed His human Church
Christ married Her with cry of dreadful pain

22 and loss of life. To keep Her true to him,
    Providence sent the Church two princely men.
    One was for wisdom like the cherubim

25 and one whose ardour matched the seraphim
    who I will speak of first, since praise of him
    applies to both. They toiled for the same end.

28 The Porta Sole of Perugia
    faces the Apennine, whence winds blow down
    both hot and cold. Small rivers too descend,

31 surround a town where Mount Subasio
    slopes to the plain. Assisi is its name.
    A better name for it is Orient

34 for here dawned Francis, Italy's new sun.
    While still a lad he revelled in the sins
    most folk forgive the child of a rich man,

37 or even praise. He fought in petty war,
    caroused and whored, was very popular,
    then illness made him face the fact of death,

40 forced him to see he was not fit for it.
    He read what Jesus said to the rich youth
    who wanted Heaven, and knew these words were true,

43 then tried to give away the wealth he had,
    resulting in a quarrel with his dad
    because he chose a bride all wished to shun.

46 Her first spouse had been taken from her side
    over eleven hundred years before.
    Though known to famous men much earlier

(Diogenes was one who scorned a great   49
world conqueror), the proud rejected her.
None took example from her constancy.

Even Christ's mother stayed below when she   52
climbed up the Cross to share Christ's agony.
In case you cannot guess of whom I speak

the bride who Francis wed was Poverty,   55
in church renouncing his inheritance
on earth to live on just what Heaven's Dad

gives everyone who does not seek for gain.   58
With such a wife he came to love her more
and poor himself, worked hard to help the poor.

Though old companions flung mud at him,   61
his happiness and harmony moved some
of contemplative mind to emulate.

His wealthy neighbour Bernard was the first   64
to kick off shoes and follow him barefoot.
Egidius, Sylvester followed suit.

Eight others too, delighting in his bride,   67
wore rough wool robe tied with a simple cord
and did not fear the sneers of vulgar wealth.

The scorn they all found very hard to bear   70
came from those thinking them competitors
in holiness: the confirmed clergymen.

Francis and his eleven followers   73
walked forth to Rome and showed Pope Innocent
the nature of Franciscan brotherhood.

76 Thus it was tolerated by the Church,
    and when the flocks of Francis grew much more
    through missions to France, Spain and Germany

79 Pope Honorius made its status sure.
    Francis then sailed to Egypt and when there
    preached Christ until the sultan promised him

82 far better treatment of the Christian slaves,
    and in Jerusalem Christ's tomb would be
    placed firmly in Franciscan brothers' care,

85 after which he returned to Italy.
    Twixt Arno and the Tiber is a crag
    where stands the cell where Francis found good proof

88 that Jesus loved him well: on hands, feet, side
    the bloody wounds of crucifixion came.
    For two more years he bore those stigmata

91 till Christ who destined him to so much good
    disclosed that his last day was drawing near.
    He then bequeathed the poverty he'd wed

94 to all his brothers, begging them always
    to love her faithfully. Then from the ground
    (he had rejected any other bier)

97 his ardent soul rose up to Paradise.
    Consider now which colleague is most fit
    to help God keep Saint Peter's boat afloat

100 on troubled seas under our stormy skies.
    Surely my own patriarch Dominic!
    His followers carry good merchandise

although too many wander far away   103
to fields remote from where he guided them,
thus yielding to their fold much less sweet milk.

Some dutifully keep their shepherd's path,   106
so few their cowls require but little cloth.
Now know my meaning when you heard me say

there is good fattening unless we stray."   109

12: Of Dominic

1   And when that holy flame said his last word
the shining chorus circled once again,
and I beheld that now surrounding it

4   a ring of other shining souls revolved.
The outer ring echoed the middle one
in colours of the purest harmony.

7   As sunbursts pierce the clouds after a storm
in double rainbows they enhaloed us,
also in dancing movements and sweet song.

10   And then this festival of light and sound
suddenly paused. From one new vivid heart
came speech. Like compass needle to the pole

13   I turned to that bright soul and heard it say:
"A love of justice forces me to speak
of Dominic. You heard Aquinas say

16   for wisdom he was near the cherubim.
Because Aquinas, a Dominican,
praised Francis to the height where he belongs

19   it is but right that I, a Franciscan,
equally celebrate Saint Dominic.
Christ made our Church to be God's force on earth.

It ended European paganism.   22
Since then its foes have been hypocrisy
(which Francis fought) and heresy.

Heads of some well-fed priests had grown so thick   25
they did not clearly understand Christ's laws
or know exactly what heresy was.

Dominic came to teach these things, and did.   28
This mighty athlete for the Christian cause,
this hero keen to counteract God's foes,

came from a tiny village in Castile   31
near the Atlantic shore. His mother dreamed
when he was in her womb she bore a dog

with flaming torch in mouth to kindle faith,   34
then his godmother dreamed before baptism
a guiding star was glowing on his brow.

She chose a Christian name whose greatest part 37
is Latin word for master: *dominus*,
so he became a master gardener

tending the vines of Christ. When infant, he   40
stared at the ground, as often pondering
Christ's early words, *seek for God's kingdom first.*

His father's name, Felici, meant delight;   43
his mother Giovanna's grace of God.
Suitable names! Their son became a priest

renowned for honesty and industry   46
not rich by mastery of canon laws
but earning Heaven's bread: enough to feed

49 his strength by working for the poor and weak,
in wasted fields where vines were withering
because they'd been in need of proper care.

52 Then he approached the highest priest of all,
one much less friendly to the upright poor
than better popes who filled that seat before.

55 He did not want wealth left for pious use,
or for a chance to rob from charities
or for a more exalted job. He begged

58 for leave to preach against the erring world
and use both learning and his holy zeal
to combat false beliefs where these prevailed.

61 Permission thus requested was received.
Like torrent pouring down a mountainside
he and his preachers flung themselves upon

64 thickets and undergrowths of heresy,
using most force in scouring up the roots
where they had clung most deep. He is the source

67 of many pure streams watering young shoots
and keeping faith's Catholic garden green.
Men like Saint Dominic compose the rings

70 shining like double garlands in this sun,
or like two wheels on which our chariot,
the Church, should run when strife is overcome.

73 Both deserve praise that Thomas Aquinas
politely gave Francis before I spoke.
I am the soul of Bonaventura,

once head of Francis' order who well knew   76
honour and wealth are traps we can avoid.
I fear that sorrow reaches me in Heaven.

My order now is troubled by a schism   79
for some now bind themselves to poverty
too painfully for many to endure;

some find the right track hard so go too slow   82
retarding men who walk behind their back.
These shirk our rule; the former narrow it.

Read our book carefully and I admit   85
you will find pages truly written with
I keep those rules of Francis I have vowed,

yet foul weeds sprout within our field of corn.   88
When it is time to bring the harvest in,
how loudly they will shout as they complain

of reapers who won't garner them as grain!   91
I'll introduce you to my circle now.
Illuminato and Augustine were

first barefoot brethren to become God's friends.   94
See Hugh of Paris, theologian;
two Peters next of Troyes and of Spain.

The first expounded Bible history,   97
the Spaniard made the use of logic plain
in twelve small books before elected pope.

Now two who preached on sins of royalty —   100
Nathan rebuked David of Israel,
Empress Eudoxia winced from the tongue

103 of Chrysostom or Golden Mouth who was
    Byzantine patriarch. Anselm came next,
    England's Archbishop representing Rome,

106 who argued with its kings; then Donatus,
    grammarian and teacher of that art
    on which speech, writing, law depend, then next

109 Rabanus the German Latinist and
    commentator. Lastly, here at my side
    shines Abbot Joachim, who drew divine

112 prophecies from Saint John's Apocalypse.
    And now I must acknowledge yet again
    the splendid courtesy of Aquinas

115 to saintly Francis, my own paladin,
    which moved me here to say the good I know
    about the equally great Dominic,

118 who also showed how to live free of sin."

13: Sun Wisdom

To comprehend, though faintly, what came next, 1
keep as you read this firm in your mind's eye
each image as if chiselled upon rock.

Remember all the biggest, brightest stars 4
that, piercing misty vapour in the air,
illuminate the deepest midnight sky.

Think of that constellation, the Great Bear 7
swinging in so much space round the Pole Star
no part is hidden by the highest hills.

The axle of the turning universe 10
ends in that Pole. Between it and the Bear
a smaller constellation swings. Think now,

both galaxies made of the brightest stars 13
and in concentric spheres, not simple rings,
and oppositely moving round we two.

My words can only show this state of things 16
as a full noonday sun reveals itself
reflected in a muddy shallow pool.

They tell you nothing of that golden sound, 19
that holy anthem all those wise stars sang,
grander than paeans to Apollo were.

22 That anthem glorified the Three-in-One,
divine and natural and singular
united in our Jesus Christ, God's son.

25 Their singing, circling halted yet once more.
The lights were pleased to stop and tutor me
as he who'd told me of God's poorest man

28 (Saint Francis of Assisi) spoke again.
"One of your doubts about this company
has been resolved. Sweet charity requires

31 I solve the next you formed too hastily
in thinking I called Solomon wiser
than greater men we both revere. Attend!

34 All things that cannot die and all that can
are ideas that our loving God pours out
in torrents of creative light, whose rays

37 first form angelic potencies and then
Nature reflects them in her elements
so they appear as bodies among men.

40 While making visible divine ideas
Nature's hand often shakes, so what she makes
is not quite right. The living upon earth

43 must propagate themselves by birth or seed,
and doing so, incline to accidents
obstructing slightly Heaven-sent design.

46 Thus, better and worse fruit may grow on trees
of the same kind, while similar folk show
astonishing varieties of mind,

but Highest Love created by Itself   49
two prototypes, because a living man
was first perfected from earth's dust, and then

a second made within a virgin's womb.   52
You heard how Adam's side bestowed a rib
taken to make his bride, the lovely Eve

whose appetite for fruit led to disgrace.   55
When a spear-point stabbed our Redeemer's side
the dear cost of that sin at last was paid.

Adam and Christ were perfect men and so   58
none others were as good, I quite agree,
but think of Solomon and what he said

when God enquired, "What should I give to thee?" 61
Solomon prayed for knowledge to rule well.
I only meant that in wise government

no men or kings could rise higher than he   64
and most are far below. Remember this!
Be slow in making judgements, like those men

imagining great harvests when ripe corn   67
stands in their fields before storms lay it low.
A winter briar bush showing bare spikes

may in the spring months bloom into a rose.   70
I saw a ship sail swiftly across seas
then suffer wreck on entering a port.

When in church we see one rob the poor-box,   73
one contribute alms, do not judge at all.
One may be Hell-bound, one for Paradise.

The first one may repent, the second fall."   76

14: From Sun to Mars

1   Water contained by bowl flows out to rim
    if pebble is dropped in. When rim is struck
    the water ripples back. The flow of words

4   from shining Thomas reached our ears then stopped.
    As if struck by a thought, Beatrice spoke.
    "Dear Sir, more words are needed by this man

7   who does not know what he should ask. I do.
    All Paradise is made of light, souls too.
    On the last day who must unite again

10   with their old fleshly bodies raised from dust,
    even their eyes? How will they see without
    (at least at first) intolerable pain?"

13   This question, eager and devout, aroused
    in the wise stars a storm of tuneful mirth.
    With swifter melody they danced in form

16   of blossoms, falling snow, butterfly wings,
    for with these words I try and fail to tell
    the lovely, wondrous things this dance conveyed

19   until Saint Thomas said, "The miracle
    of Resurrection painlessly restores
    all the First Will intended us to be,

with bodies free as minds too seldom are,   22
except for those of the angelic kinds,
and of Our Father, only One In Three,

Eternal, Natural and Singular   25
replenishing, refreshing such as we."
Then the full chorus of the solar choirs

sang what the sainted Thomas said three times,   28
sang it so beautifully that the sound
will satisfy the ferventest desires

of all who come to merit Paradise.   31
From out the central globe spoke Solomon,
his voice as archangelically soft

as if announcing Mary's pregnancy.   34
"When bodies finally complete our souls
we will surpass in brightness what you see,

as flaming coals surpass black stones from mines.   37
And yet we shall not be consumed because
God's virtue wills we share in His delight."

So quick were both the choirs to sing *Amen*   40
I knew they longed to have their bodies back
not for themselves alone. They wished to see

mothers, fathers, more they had dearly loved   43
in times before they were immortal flames.
And then I saw beyond the outer sphere

a new horizon form of equal stars   46
like galaxies seen here when day is done,
but these were shining round our undimmed sun!

49 The brilliance was more than I could bear,
banishing both my sight and memory.
Only the fair and smiling Beatrice

52 survives from later visions of the sun.
We reached a higher zone of Paradise
when I at last recovered use of sight.

55 The planet with the glow of ruddy light
which to the heathen indicated war,
kindled in me a need for sacrifice.

58 In words of heartfelt silent inner prayer
(the only speech all share) I pled with Christ
to take this thing I am, and fought to give

61 with every living particle of will,
then found my offering acceptable.
The Crucifix appeared within that star,

64 its beams from side to side, from foot to top
wide as a crossroads made of the same stuff
as, bridging the night sky, that thoroughfare

67 from pole to pole – the gleaming Milky Way.
This cross so flamed forth Christ, my memory
defeats my skill to speak of it, but all

70 who lift the cross of Christ and follow Him
will forgive me for what I cannot say
about His vision flashing in the dawn.

73 From arm to arm, summit to base and back
lights travelled, sparkling as they met and passed,
some swift or slow, some dazzling, and some dim

because they sparkled less but happiness   76
was equally in all. Harp and viola
combine so well we cannot tell apart

what each gives melody. The moving lights   79
gave out a hymn whose words I did not catch
and yet the whole conveyed *arise and win*

so sweetly none had ever bound my soul   82
in such enchanting chains of lovely sound,
which sight of Beatrice did not prevent,

whose beauty grew more pure with each ascent.   85

15: Martial Hero

1   Bad manners grow from greedy selfishness,
    as courtesy reflects Christ's charity
    which, as we know, is kindness to the weak.

4   I needed silence if required to speak
    and so it came. The choirs of Paradise
    silenced their song when, like a shooting star

7   down gloaming sky, from right arm of the cross
    yet linked to it by arc of finer fire
    a light swept down to join me at the foot.

10 It greeted me with the same welcoming
    that Virgil tells us in *The Aeneid*
    the soul of dead Anchises gave his son

13 who, living, met him in Elysium.
    "O my own blood! O wondrous grace of God
    that Paradise will open to you twice!"

16 The light said that. Amazed, I turned my eyes
    to Beatrice again, whose smile was such
    I fully knew how blessèd I'd become.

19 And then, although the sound was ecstasy,
    the light said things I could not comprehend.
    Their meaning was too great till heat of love

cooled down enough, letting it condescend   22
to sentences of much more common sense.
"Divine foreknowledge we in Heaven share

has kept me long expecting this delight.   25
Holy the guide who dressed you in such wings
as raise you to this height! You rightly think

I know your thoughts, so do not ask my name,   28
or why my joy appears much greater than
the others in this sphere. You are about

to satisfy my thirst to share the bliss   31
of perfect truthfulness. Ask what you wish."
Encouragement from smiling Beatrice

gave me the confidence to boldly say,   34
"Just as the sun's ray pours out equally
both warmth and light, you equally possess

love and intelligence, which mortals lack.   37
I am still mortal. My ability
cannot support my will. Not tongue but heart

declares my depth of gratitude for this   40
paternal welcoming. I beg you now,
O jewel in the Cross and Crown of Christ

say who you are." "O branch I greet with joy,   43
I am your root, your ancestor," said he.
"My son became your great-great-great-granddad

who has been trudging for a century   46
round Purgatory's ring where pride is purged.
Pray to reduce his toil when back on earth.

49 We knew a Florence that, seen from afar,
did not appear to outshine Rome as much
as one day it will look a great deal worse.

52 Back then our town was peaceful, sober, chaste,
filled smaller ground. No wife or daughter wore
jewellery, embroidered gown, rich stuff seen

55 before the wearers. No dad lived in dread
of baby girls growing too old to wed
before he got enough gold for dowry.

58 People were buried in their native soil –
no exiled owner left an empty house.
No families had rooms they did not use

61 or houses like the palaces of kings.
Nobility dressed plain. Our honoured knight
good Bellincion wore a leather suit

64 and had a wife with clean unpainted face.
Wives were lucky. Husbands did not desert
the marriage bed to trade abroad for years.

67 Mothers rocked cradles, soothing infant fears
by crooning songs that pleased themselves and dads,
then later, spinning thread, told older bairns

70 brave tales of Trojans; how they fought and spread
to Italy, Fiesole and Rome;
then told of Cincinnatus and Lucrece,

73 who both chose death rather than break an oath.
Kids would have marvelled more to hear about
those who now dominate Florence's state:

corrupted lawyers! Blatant prostitutes!   76
To life in Florence as the town was then,
with lovely streets, good neighbours, honest men,

my mother no doubt bore me crying out   79
Mary, as women do when giving birth.
Then in our ancient baptistry the priest

christened and called me Cacciaguida.   82
My wife came from the valley of the Po
bringing your surname, Alighieri.

I followed Conrad, Emperor who led   85
the next Crusade to free Jerusalem:
was knighted by him for my part in fight

to free Christ's sepulchre from pagan hands.   88
We lost, as Christendom is not – *should be* –
united by the popes. Death shifted me

into this perfect bliss called Martyrdom."   91

16: Old Families

1 How daft you are, great pride in noble birth!
On earth I knew proud men deformed by you
and here in Paradise you ruled my mood.

4 Since evil could not influence my soul
I freely gloried in my noble birth.
That Cacciaguida died on a Crusade

7 as many others did is widely known.
How wonderful to find my ancestor
had once been knighted by the Emperor!

10 Pride is a splendid robe. Alas, it shrinks
as time goes round us with its snipping shears
cutting off hems, while pride makes us sew on

13 new widths of extra cloth. I spoke again
addressing him as *Sire*, once common speech
but now a title fallen out of date.

16 My lady stood apart, but near, and smiled
reminding me of something I had read.
When Lancelot was courting Guinevere

19 a waiting woman who was standing near,
hearing what hinted at adultery,
gave a wee warning cough. My lady's smile

suggested that *ahem*, but still I spoke.   22
"Dear Sire, you are my great progenitor!
Sire, you embolden me to speak my mind,

for Sire, you lift me up so high I feel   25
much more than me! So many happy streams
flow down into my mind, I do not know

how I can entertain them and not drown!   28
So please, dear Sire and source of all my blood,
when were *you* born? Who were *your* ancestors?

What people flourished in your days of youth?   31
I know that pagan Florence worshipped Mars,
then took the Baptist John as Patron Saint

and shepherd too. How many were his flock?   34
Which families were worthy of respect?"
As puff of breath makes red-hot coal flare up,

so did my grandsire brighten at my prayer.   37
His voice grew gentler, sweeter as he said,
"From when the Virgin heard she was with child

to when my sainted mother gave me birth   40
Mars, moving round the starry zodiac,
had told eleven-hundred-eighty years.

I and my forefathers were born between   43
the Ponte Vecchio and Baptistry.
Where they came from before I do not know.

When Florence was a fifth its present size   46
they carried weapons to defend the town
in time of war. I know their blood was pure

49 like all in Florence then, labourers too.
None had been tainted by their intercourse
with Campi, Certaldo and Fighine.

52 If kept beyond our walls these hives of boors
would not have their offspring's offsprings knocking
hard at your doors, if not at home inside.

55 No stinking clowns out of Aguglione
and Signa could be swindling or preside
over Florentine citizens today.

58 The priesthood who, of all the men on earth
should most uphold the laws that Caesar made
that Europe might be unified in peace,

61 undid the ties of right authority.
They let some people become Florentine
who live by lending, borrowing and pawns.

64 You have a banker who, were justice done,
would be returned to Semifonte where
his grandsire was a beggar in the streets.

67 Good counts would still own Montemurlo;
the Cerchi, Acone; the Buondelmonte,
Valdegrieve. Admitting strangers begins

70 municipal decline, as too much food
destroys a body's health. Blind bulls fall
heavier than sightless lambs. A swordsman,

73 neat and trim, can cut down five obese
oponents. Think of Urbisaglia,
of Luni too, cities that disappeared,

and how Chiusi and Senigallia   76
are following. People and cities die.
It is not strange great families fade too.

Don't think it marvellous if now I name   79
great Florentines whose fame is dimmed by time.
I saw the Ughi, Greci, Ormanni,

the Filippi and Alberichi too: 82
illustrious, though near extinction then.
Others I saw, ancient but also great:

del Arca, Sannella, Soldanieri,   85
Ardinghi and Bostichi, also the
Ravignani, famed now for perfidy

soon to eclipse that line. Among them was   88
Count Guido, descended from the splendid
Bellincion. Della Pressa by then

knew how to rule. Galigaio wore   91
a knight's sword. So did Galli, Sacchetti
and a few more who bore the Pigli arms.

So did the cheat who falsified the weights   94
for salt he sold. The Calfucci forebears
had become great. I saw pride bring them low.

When three gold balls flourished over Florence   97
Sizii, Arrigucci were officers.
So were grandsires of those who, noticing

vacancies in the Church, fill them, grow rich   100
– mean men of base blood, dragons to the weak,
lambs to those showing teeth, or a full purse!

103 That crew was rising. The Caponsacco
    from Fiesole was in our market-place.
    Giuda and Infangato had become

106 respected citizens, Argenti too,
    though Ubertino Donato was peeved
    when his father-in-law made *him* their kin

109 by wedding his wife's sister onto one.
    I'll tell you something strange. Those inner walls
    the ancient Romans built were entered once

112 by a gate named after della Pera;
    people forgotten now. Then everyone
    who bore the arms of Tuscan marquis Hugh

115 were Tory through and through, although today
    one, Guiano della Bella, is a Whig
    cheered by the mob. The Gualterotti and

118 Importuni still had not sunk so low
    as to become the tradesmen that you know.
    The Borgo district would have stayed at peace

121 had the Buondelmonte not arrived,
    that family from which your tears have sprung
    from just resentment of the death it brought,

124 ending your chances of a happy life.
    O Buondelmonte, you were wrong to jilt
    she you had sworn to wed, and take instead

127 a daughter of the Donati. Many
    now sorrowful would have led happy lives
    if you had drowned before you reached our town.

The family whose daughter you jilted   130
slaughtered you fittingly on Arno's bridge
beside that wasted stone, statue of Mars,

thus starting endless Whig and Tory wars.   133
My tranquil days were passed before our strife
became continual, but then our flag

(never taken in battle by a foe)   136
became two: Tory lilies on white ground;
Whig lilies upon red. This fatal split

led to more bloodshed, many thousands dead."   139

17: Dante's Future

1   That shining soul my very great grandsire
could read my mind. My wish was now to hear
what Florence held for me when I returned,

4   but he was silent. I began to fear
this was a thing he wished me not to know.
I looked to Beatrice who gently said,

7   "He wants to satisfy your thirst but first,
to prove you understand what you desire,
say what it is in words that make it clear."

10   I cried, "Dear root of me, your intellect
has soared to such a height, you share with God
His view of time past, present and to come.

13   If I should live to be three score and ten
I have run halfway through my time on earth.
When deep with Virgil in the cone of Hell

16   and up Mount Purgatory, I heard tell
dark prophecies about my future years.
They told me these would bring much suffering.

19   Let fuller knowledge please reduce their sting,
for that is what I pray you give me now.
Forewarned is forearmed, we in Florence say."

Unlike those riddling oracles struck dumb   22
by Christ's triumphant Crucifixion
what he now spoke had no obscurity.

"Do not believe your future agony   25
is willed by God because it is foreseen.
He no more plans the world's contingencies

than an observing eye moves ships at sea.   28
You know how slander drove Hippolytus
from his Athenian home. For Whigs like you

the very same is being planned in Rome.   31
Of course the injured parties will be blamed,
though vengeance one day will reveal the truth.

The first pains that you feel will be the worst: 34
the agony of leaving all you love,
eating the tasteless bread of charity,

learning how steep are stairs you do not own.   37
Heavier too will be the company
of those also expelled, a senseless crew

vilely denouncing you. Their vicious fuss   40
will grow as brutal as notorious.
None will believe them; fame will make you be

a political party of just one,   43
and favourite guest of della Scala,
Lombard Count of Verona. His regard

will give what you most need before you ask.   46
You will know his brother, born below Mars
and now a child. After the Papacy

49 moves to Avignon, and French Pope Clement
   fools the Emperor Henry, you will see
   that boy heroic, fearing neither wealth

52 nor toil, his generosity so great
   his foes will praise it while he makes beggars
   change place with millionaires. You will see this

55 and not say how you knew it would be so."
   He said more, which only those who see
   them happen can possibly believe, adding,

58 "My dear son, this explains the worst rumours
   of the foul snares awaiting you in years
   that are to come. Don't envy Florentines

61 able to stay at home. You'll live to see
   them suffering for their foul perfidy."
   That shining soul fell silent, having shown

64 the woven pattern of my tapestry.
   I needed better news from He who sees
   all that exists, and rightly wills and loves.

67 "Father," said I unhappily, "since now
   loss of my dearest home is known to me,
   advise me how to keep the place I've won

70 in people's minds by my poetic song.
   In Hell, and on that Hill my lady's eyes
   have raised me from, I learned many things that,

73 immortalised in art, are bound to hurt.
   I am a timid friend of truth, so fear
   danger from folk who want their crimes forgot."

The light from which my grandsire smiled now blazed   76
like golden mirror in the brightest sun.
He said, "Consciences dark with their own sin

or shame at another's guilt will indeed   79
feel pain, but do not nurse hypocrisy!
Make the truth plain! Let them scratch where they itch.

Your verses may taste bad at first; digested   82
they will be nourishing. Write like the wind,
hitting high mountains hardest. What more

can poet do? That is why you have been shown   85
only the famous down below in Hell
and up Mount Purgatory. Folk ignore

examples set by those they don't know well."   88

18: From Mars to Jupiter

1 My ancestor, reflecting Paradise,
seemed in a pleasant dwam. I, blending thoughts
bitter and sweet, grew gradually calm.

4 My guide leading me Godward said, "Time now
to change your mind. Think, I am leading you to
He who heals the pains of every wrong."

7 I turned toward her lovely voice and saw
more love within her eyes than I can tell,
not just because I distrust words I use,

10 but all I felt in Heaven has grown dim.
I only knew, gazing on Beatrice,
this was the only thing I wished to do,

13 when smiling she said, "Hear your good grandsire!
Learn that my eyes don't hold all Paradise."
As strong emotion will transform a face

16 new brilliance in my grandsire's vivid light
told me that there was more he wished to say.
"In this fifth sphere the tree with living top

19 is always fruitful, never sheds its leaves,
which are heroic spirits from the earth.
Your verses must be brightened by their fame.

Watch the crossbeam on which our Saviour hung. 22
Each soul I name will glow like lightning there."
When he said, "Joshua," the lightning flashed,

nor did I hear the word before the light. 25
As he said, "Maccabaeus," one light spun
fast as a top whipped into ecstasy.

My eyes pursued like falcons in their flight 28
Charlemagne, Roland, Robert Guiscard,
Renuard the Saracen Crusader,

Duke Godfrey King of Jerusalem and 31
William of Orange. Other fighting saints
also drew my attention through the cross,

and then my grandsire swooped back up to join 34
these mighty glories in their harmonies.
Looking back to Beatrice for a sign

of what came next, I saw her eyes so clear, 37
so joyful, she surpassed in loveliness
even herself before. I felt as free

as man in whom virtue and wisdom grew, 40
or a good woman freed from wrongful shame.
We swung in wider arcs among white lights

of the vaster, higher sphere called Jupiter. 43
Language commanded in this temperate star,
since words themselves make shared love possible

for folk not brutes. Good Latin was the speech 46
of this sixth planet, used by the Roman
Empire, Catholic Church, Law, Sciences.

49 I saw lights soaring like great flocks of birds
and forming shapes that, flowing through themselves,
became the letters of the alphabet.

52 In swathes of living light they shaped a **D**,
then **I**, then **L**. Singing and soaring they
suddenly ceased flight and silence ensued.

55 O sacred Pegasus! You Christian steed
that raises humble souls to genius,
you true imagination that creates

58 vigour and unity in men and states!
Let me spell out the letters, one by one,
as they appeared, and so pronounce their sense.

61 I read **DILIGITE JUSTITIAM
QUI JUDICATIS TERRAM**, words which mean
Love justice, you who judge the earth! Lights then

64 congregated within that final **M**,
making all Jupiter a galaxy
of gold and silver jewels. After, between

67 the two sharp summits of the **M** I saw
thousands of other lights descend, settle
and sing (I think) of God convening them.

70 Like sparks that leap from burning log when kicked
– sparks in which fools see auguries – these lights,
both large and small, rose up between those peaks.

73 When each had settled in its place I saw
the shape of an enormous eagle's head,
sides of the **M** its downward sweeping wings,

a shape designed by He who taught each bird
the way to build a nest. These blessèd souls
by movements made a lily's shape appear

within the eagle's breast. O splendid star!
How many and how bright the gems of light
making it plain justice is consequence

of the high Paradise You decorate.
I pray the Mind that started everything
will mend the Papacy broken in two.

From there comes the black smoke that dims Your beams
thus leading Christians astray. You must be
furious again to see Your temple

plundered and changed by thieves into a den
where Salvation is sold and bought for gold.
Popes should not make war with spear and sword,

in competitions to command more men
and tax more land, refusing Holy Bread
due to all Christened souls, in spite of God.

You Popes who write now only to condemn,
should start believing Saints Peter and Paul
are still in Heaven and still judging you.

Well may you say, "My heart belongs to John,
the saint whose head Salome once danced off.
Forget the Fisherman, forget Paul too!

Give me gold coins stamped with the Baptist John!"

19: The Eagle Speaks

1 In front of me appeared with open wings
    that great bird made of congregated souls,
    each a wee ruby with a star inside.

4 What I tell now no tongue has ever told
    and none has written down. No one before
    ever conceived of such a splendid thing.

7 I saw and heard the beak begin to speak,
    say *I* and *mine* while meaning *we* and *ours*.
    "For being just and merciful," it said,

10 "I once possessed a glory none surpassed.
    Though rulers praise my memory on earth
    none have continued my great story there."

13 I cried, "O everlasting fruit of bliss,
    you represent a Justice higher still,
    yet you reflect it pure and know my mind.

16 Please feed the hunger that has famished me.
    How keen I am to hear you end the doubt
    upsetting my digestion many years."

19 Like an unhooded falcon flapping wings
    and preening them in readiness for flight
    so did that unity of noble souls,

then it spoke out: "Turning his compasses   22
to draw the ring that holds all space and time,
the Universal Architect made no part

of the diversity within its bounds   25
greater than His creating Mind and Word.
As proof, the foremost intellect He made,

thinking itself His equal, would not wait   28
to be ripened by His gift of light. Pride –
overweening pride – led Satan to rebel,

expel himself from height of Paradise.   31
All natures less than God are far too small
to measure the Eternal Infinite.

Each thought is one ray of the Divine Mind   34
but none can comprehend all other rays
except by basking in their plenitude.

Believe that ignorance and sin obscure   37
most things you cannot understand. You think,
Indians live who never heard Christ's name,

yet guided by straight reason, do no wrong,   40
like some born before God was crucified.
What justice can condemn such souls to Hell?

That thought came when you could not see beyond   43
the hills around your town, so could not know
anything about those in Asia

more than a thousand miles away, or guess   46
how God will deal with them. His Gospel tells
everything a good soul needs to know

49 for living sinlessly. Thinking further
can show His wonders for your admiration.
Apparent contradictions in His schemes

52 come by speculation further knowledge
will solve, either before or after death.
They cannot blight an honest Christian life."

55 That glowing heraldry that spread respect
for Roman government over the globe
soared round above my head, as mother stork

58 will fly in circles over a young chick
gazing lovingly up from the warm nest
where it has just been fed. The eagle sang

61 a hymn whose words I did not know, then said,
"Just as my song is meaningless to you,
God's justice is beyond men's reasoning.

64 None rise up here who have not faith in Christ
before or since they nailed Him to that tree,
but now we hear too many cry, *Christ! Christ!*

67 who on Judgement Day will be deeper damned
than Africans who never heard His name.
What will Asians think when they hear read out

70 the deeds of Christian kings? How Prague was made
a wilderness by Emperor Albert?
How the French King, debasing currency,

73 brought poverty to both banks of the Seine?
There shall be seen arrogance maddening
English and Scots who battle constantly

across the border nature built for them.   76
They will discover Naples' crippled king,
his single virtue and his thousand sins;

know too why crimes of the Sicilian king   79
must be described in shorthand, to save space,
and how they have dishonoured good King

William, their noble relative. Kings of   82
Norway and Portugal seem just as bad
as he of Serbia whose forged coins spread

distrust of Venice's minted silver.   85
O Happy Hungary if Martel's son
saves you from such misrule! Happy Navarre

if mountains can protect you from the French   88
and their king's foul stench! And you can see how
miserable Cyprus is, like all states

or islands that have Frenchmen as their mates!"   91

20: The Eagle's Eye

1   The sun that fills our eyes with daily light
    curves upward through the sky and down again,
    then passes underground, and it is night

4   when multitudes of galaxies appear.
    This change from one to many brilliances
    happened when, ceasing speech, that single voice

7   became a mighty choir singing a hymn.
    At times, O love, you're only seen in smiles.
    How glorious you sounded in that song!

10 I cannot now recall that harmony
    of holy thought, but noticed when the gems
    enriching the sixth sphere altered their tune,

13 became a murmuring of waters like
    many clear streams trickling from rock to rock.
    As a lute's plucked strings resonate, I heard

16 murmurs climb the bird's hollow neck until
    articulate within the beak again
    they spoke these words my heart hungered to hear:

19 "Look closely to the part of me that sees!
    Of all the fires I use to make my form
    these sparkling in my head are surely best.

The pupil of my eye was he whose Psalms   22
truly proclaim news of the Holy Ghost.
He brought the Ark home to Jerusalem.

Five others make my eyebrow's arch. Trajan   25
is beside my beak. To the poor widow
who lost her son he was most just, and yet

damned as an infidel. Gregory's prayers   28
lifted him from Hell so he knows full well
the state of those with Jesus and without.

Hezekiah next, whose true repentance   31
after divine reproof prolonged his life.
He knows decrees eternal are unchanged

on earth when the right prayers extend our days. 34
Next, Constantine who went east, became Greek,
christened the Roman Empire, giving Rome

to the popes. Though these deeds redeemed his soul 37
too many have been ruined by the last.
See good King William on my sloping brow,

mourned by Naples and Sicily. These weep   40
under his brother Charles, son Frederick.
His shining shows that Heaven loves the just.

Who in the erring world below believes   43
that in this sphere of perfect governors
pagan Ripheus is fifth guiding light?

Virgil called him *most just of Trojan kings*.   46
His soul knew more of Divine Grace than most,
though none have sight that penetrate the whole."

49 Then suddenly the great bird seemed a lark
    soaring and singing up the face of space
    to hover silently, sweetly content,

52 a perfect image of eternal joy
    whose will allows all things that are to be.
    In my perplexity I felt like glass

55 that cannot see the colour staining it.
    Failing to wait for wisdom I cried out,
    "How *CAN* that be?" provoking a great storm,

58 a revelry of vivid flashing light.
    With even brighter eye the bird replied,
    "You see the things I show, not what they are!

61 Like those who know the names of many things,
    you cannot grasp their substances unless
    many more words are said. Strong Hope and Love

64 you met in earthly paradise with Faith.
    Faith, Hope and Love occupy Heaven, *not*
    like men invading men: Heaven invites

67 good to be part of it. You are amazed
    to see in me a Jew and pagan king,
    but death revealed their souls were Christian.

70 Their faith in Hope and Love had been so strong
    they never doubted justice could prevail
    on earth as it prevails in Paradise.

73 They prayed for that, and so for them it did.
    We, close to God, don't know all His elect –
    cannot know all He knows. This ignorance

refines us. We have always more to learn."   76
This eagle's teaching brought me to accept
my ignorance, pride's sweetest medicine,

and as he spoke each star around his eyes   79
dancingly twinkled, almost seemed to play
a fine orchestral symphony of sound

to emphasise all he was moved to say.   82

21: Saturn

1 My lady, reading worship in my eyes,
gravely regarded me and then declared,
"I must not smile. My beauty shines the more

4 at each new height we reach. If not restrained,
the blaze of it will turn you into ash
like Semelé who gazed on Jupiter,

7 or cleave you as the lightning splits a tree.
We have ascended to the seventh sphere –
Saturn, beneath the Lion galaxy.

10 Waken the mind behind your eyes! Reflect
deeply the image that will now appear."
Though very sad to look away from her

13 it was a pleasure to obey. I saw
deep in the crystal circling our earth
a ladder, golden, flashing in the sun

16 to such great height my eyes could see no top,
and on it moved so many splendid forms
all lights in Paradise appeared thereon.

19 And as at daybreak flocks of birds will fly
higher to warm their feathers in the sun,
and scattering while others flutter down,

I saw one settle on a nearby step,   22
seeming to grow more bright with love for me!
Or so I thought, but did not dare to speak

till Beatrice said, "Say what you desire."   25
Said I, "Although unworthy of reply,
since I am granted leave to speak, say why

silence is so profound at this great height?   28
Heavens below are jubilant with sound."
The light replied, "Your ears are as mortal

as your sight. Your deafness to our music   31
is from the same reason why you must not
here be allowed to see Beatrice smile.

I have descended, cloaked within my light   34
to welcome you, guided by charity
that rules, as you perceive, the universe."

"O holy lamp," said I, "indeed I see   37
how free love here serves the Eternal Mind.
I do not understand why you alone

are commanded to speak with me." At once   40
round at centre the light spun like a millstone
or Catherine wheel and said, "Divine light

focused on me adds to my radiance,   43
but seraphs who directly look on God
won't answer questions that created minds

can't grasp. When back on earth tell people that   46
what here is clarity seems smoke down where
too few have lifted themselves Heavenward."

49 Checked by these words, I humbly asked his name.
"Within Italian shores near your home town
are crags so high thunder sounds far below.

52 They form a ridge called Caria on which
a hermitage is built. There I served God
so constantly, in contemplative mood

55 in heat or cold my need of food was small.
That cloister raised for God good crops of souls –
now it sends none, and soon will be condemned.

58 Named Peter Damian, then called to Rome,
I became Cardinal where hats now pass
from bad to even worse, so signed my name

61 Peter Sinner, to remind me when priests
were barefoot, thin, begged bread at any inn.
Pastors are now too fat to stand without

64 one on each side and one holding his train.
Their fur cloaks hide palfreys on which they ride,
two beasts beneath one skin. How long must we

67 endure such sin?" He paused as bright wee globes
came wheeling down from step to step, shouting
words meaningless to me but so intense

70 their clamour fast annihilated sense.

22: Saint Benedict

Slowly my sense returned. Like a hurt child   1
I turned at once to she I trusted most:
my Beatrice. She calmed with kindly words

the trembling caused by that wild shout and said, 4
"Know you are in the sky of holiness –
pure Paradise. One cry unstrung your nerve.

How would you be if the full choir had sung?   7
Or had I smiled in my new ecstasy?
You did not hear the prayer within that cry,

or know the vengeance it was calling down   10
on those deserving that, which you will see
before you die. Neither too soon or slow,

sinners must feel the weight of Heaven's doom. 13
Now gaze around you at the company
of contemplative souls who learned to look

lovingly upon God's full radiance."   16
I obeyed, saw a hundred vivid globes
sharing the glory of their brilliance.

Halfway between desire and modesty   19
I stood, afraid to speak, tried not to say
questions that might have caused immense offence.

22 The biggest globe among these glowing pearl
then granted what I lacked the guts to ask,
saying, "If you knew that we like to help

25 asking would be no task. Not to delay
your journey on the upward track, I shall
answer the simple query you hold back.

28 The Abbey of Cassino on a hill
was pagan shrine until I carried up
the name of Jesus Christ, who died to teach

31 all people how to live. God's grace was with me.
Many heeded, left their false creed and I
baptised them in Christ's name, and two became

34 these great and Christian contemplative souls,
Makarios of Alexandria,
founder of monasteries in the east,

37 and Romualdus, stern reformer of
my holy order here, with more who stayed
strictly within their cloisters saying mass

40 nor strayed from duties of unselfish prayer."
Said I, "Your kindly speech so full of love
gives me a confidence that grows, unfolds

43 like petals in a rose. Perhaps too bold,
I beg a favour. May I see your face?"
He said, "Yes, at last in the highest place

46 where everything we want will be revealed
as perfect, whole, and outside time and space.
That sphere does not revolve around a pole.

This ladder reaches it, and that is why   49
the very top is far beyond your sight.
Patriarch Jacob glimpsed that summit once

laden with angels. None on earth below   52
now lift a foot to climb. The rules I wrote
for monks who followed me are wasted ink.

Monte Cassino is a den of thieves   55
whose robes now stink like sacks of rotten grain.
Even a moneylender can't offend

God like a lazy monk who spends on kin   58
and luxury and prostitute the cash
our Kirk collects to feed the destitute.

So weak is mortal flesh that, starting well,   61
good conduct hardly ever lasts for more
than oak trees need to grow new acorn crops.

No gold or silver helped Saint Peter found   64
our Roman Kirk. My order grew and spread
by fasts and prayers. Francis wed Poverty.

Now no Franciscans do, and thus you see   67
how white transforms to black. God saved the Jews
from Pharaoh's wrath by a dry path across

the Red Sea's bed, reversed the Jordan's flow.   70
Today our Kirk needs miracles like these."
So spoke Saint Benedict, moving away

to join his company who suddenly,   73
as if swept up by tempest, soared above.
She I love made a sign that overcame

76 my nature so completely that I too
went flying up that gold stair to the stars.
Nothing on earth was quick enough to match

79 the swiftness of our flight. When purged of sin
that chains me to the earth, how I will love
to soar in Paradise again! None pull

82 a finger faster from a flame than I
sprang into that part of the zodiac,
that constellation where knowledge and thought

85 are nourished by the starry Twins. Their rays
mingled with sunlight shone upon my birth
when I first tasted Tuscan air. Dear Twins,

88 I owe my genius to you! It was
my birthday when I reached your zone. I felt
as if coming home, and prayed you for strength

91 to undertake this great work calling me.
Said Beatrice, "A glad host soon arrives
in this triumphant air, to be received

94 gladly, with clear eyes. First exercise yours.
Look back and down. See what I raised you from."
My gaze plunged down through seven planets' rings

97 to that low thing, our queer wee comic earth
at which I smiled, now knowing thought deserved
much higher things. The moon, daughter of God,

100 appeared pure disc, recalling how wrongly
I'd explained her spots. I saw her siblings –
Mercury, Venus, Sun, Mars, Jupiter –

all tempered by old Saturn's gravity.   103
Their magnitudes and speeds and inclinations
were seen by me, and how they altered climes,

weather and tide for earth's poor folk who live   106
on coast and plain and mountainside. Meanwhile
I soared on high with the immortal Twins

then gazed into the eyes of my fair guide.   109

23: The Fixed Stars

1 As mother bird among the leaves she loves
   nests all night long upon her brood of chicks
   then wakes to watch the sky for dawn of day

4 when she will fly to seek their nourishment
   to fill each gaping beak, so Beatrice
   stood gazing at the height of firmament

7 where the sun seems to move most slow. I saw
   she looked for something new and good; what thing
   I did not know till suddenly the sky

10 was glorified by splendour flooding in.
    She cried, "O see the host of souls Christ won!
    His harvest from the virtues of the spheres!"

13 I can't find words for the serenity
    of bliss we both enjoyed at what appeared.
    As in a deep blue night the full round moon

16 outshines a myriad of stars, I saw
    a thousand thousand lights kindled by One,
    not only greater far than they combined,

19 but shining through them, lighting up all else.
    With failing sense I heard my dear love say
    "None can resist if they are overwhelmed

before the open gates of Paradise."   22
As lightning vanishes into the earth
my mind was so transported, overcome,

I do not know a thing of what came next   25
until I heard, "Open your eyes, my dear!
have they gained strength to let you see me smile?"

Like waking from a dream I can't recall   28
I faintly heard these words, then heard them clear
with gratitude I never will forget.

As to her smile, if Polyhymnia,   31
muse of sacred song, and all her sisters
of poetic art joined with me to help,

I could not say a thousandth fraction of   34
how her smile lit this part of Paradise.
My verse must leap forward upon this road.

Reader, think of my theme! One mortal man   37
carries that load. Forgive me staggering.
This journey needs a ship with daring prow

cleaving the ocean waves and captain who,   40
though weak at times, will never spare himself.
"My face should not be so enchanting that

it blinds you to the loveliest flowers   43
in garden ever lit by Christian light,"
said Beatrice. "Look at the Word of God

embodied in a rose! Virgin Mary,   46
Queen of Paradise, beside twelve lilies –
twelve apostles whose scent should draw us all

49 onto the path of truth." I turned to look.
Sometimes upon a day darkened by clouds
we see a slanting shaft of sunlight on

52 one field of lovely flowers. Now I saw
many fields of loveliness lit by rays
flashing from high above. O gracious light,

55 making them visible to one without
the strength to see their source. What courtesy!
When praying night and morn I say the name

58 of that fair virgin rose. Seeing the ray
that lit her, I then mystically knew
it had to be Archangel Gabriel.

61 And when at last I saw the magnitude
of that angelic rose, as more sublime
than all the lesser blooms beside her there

64 as she was more than those on earth below,
there came a torch descending through the sky.
Circling, it made a glory round her like

67 a halo, like a crown. Music began.
The sweetest tune that soothes us here below
would crash like thunder on the ear of those

70 who ever knew the music of that sphere,
the angels' coronation song for she,
the pure sapphire who ensapphires Heaven.

73 They sang, "O holy love surrounding joy
in womb that was the inn where came to be
One wanted by created folk who need

salvation. Now crowned the Queen of Heaven,   76
follow your Son to glory in the sphere
highest of all!" The choral music stopped.

The crowned rose vanished upward and I saw   79
all the white radiances raise their flames
like babies stretching chubby arms toward

their mother when she suckles them. They sang   82
their hymn to Heaven's Queen again. The joy
of that sweet music will be always mine.

How great are riches of delight heaped up   85
in Heaven's treasury for those on earth
who, by their exile, tears and poverty

will triumph in the total victory   88
of God, His Son and Mary, with the saints
of Old and New Testaments, and holder

of keys to the gates of so much glory.   91

24: Saint Peter

1   "O fellow diners on The Blessèd Lamb,
    both Food and Host – Host who makes sure each guest
    is satisfied, will never hunger more!

4   God's Grace permits this man to drink with us
    before his death returns him to our feast.
    He thirsts for highest truth. Please let him drink!"

7   Thus pled my loving Beatrice. These souls
    then moved like comets turning round fixed poles
    or wheels within a clock, the innermost

10 so slow they did not seem to turn at all,
    while outer ones so whirled they seemed to fly.
    I gazed amazed at wheeling meteors,

13 fast, horizontal, vertical and slow,
    a dancing revolutionary choir
    with one whose vivid flame outshone the rest.

16 Nearing, it spun three times round Beatrice
    singing a song too sweet for memory,
    nor will I try to make my pen describe

19 a vision that no artist could depict.
    The fiery soul stopped circling her and said,
    "O holy sister who can pray so well,

your loving nature draws me to your side."   22
Said she, "O guardian of Heaven's keys,
admit my lover to the height he craves,

I know that you will find him fit for it."   25
Good students do not speak till masters ask.
Gathering my wits I waited to reply.

"Good Christian, what is faith?" said he.   28
I looked to Beatrice, whose glance told me
the time had come to pour my learning out.

"May the grace letting me confess my faith   31
to the twelve apostles' chief make my words
worthy of my thought," said I. "It was you

who, helped by the pen of Paul, ordered Rome   34
along the path to Paradise. *Faith* is
reality of what we hope to see,

with *reason* for the things we've not yet seen.   37
These are faith's substance, so it seems to me."
"Yes, both are essences of faith," said he.

"Why put reason after reality?   40
Desire before convincing argument?"
Said I, "Up here great truths are clear to us,

truths that to mortal eyes appear obscure.   43
We cannot always see that God is good.
Faith in Him cannot always reason out

proof in all cases that He does things well.   46
Argument later must establish this."
He said, "If arguers below knew that,

49 no wordsmiths could confuse the faithful with
    such useless reasoning." Peter added,
    "Have you sincerely taken that to heart?

52 It is not parroted?" "These thoughts are mine,"
    I said, "new minted coins of gold, not worn,
    not clipped." He asked, "How did you come to meet

55 Beatrice, this gem who inspires your faith?"
    Said I, "The Holy Ghost, speaking in Old
    and New Testaments made me recognise

58 Beatrice at first sight." "How do you know,"
    said he, "the miracles to which these books
    testify are true?" Said I, "One miracle

61 they worked convinces me: The Kirk of Christ.
    That it is built by super-human hands
    is shown by how it still stands, propagates

64 the Word of Christ despite perverted priests.
    That miracle proves God is real and good,
    His scriptures true for they took root among

67 the persecuted poor. You were of these,
    and crucified like Jesus, yet that vine spread,
    converted Rome's Empire, a miracle

70 besides which all but one in scriptures are
    less than a hundredth part, but surely prove
    Christ's resurrection true." I said no more,

73 whereupon that whole great sphere resounded
    through its circles by singing the mighty
    anthem "Glory to God in the Highest".

After that my noble examiner   76
began again: "What you have said is right,
so now declare exactly your beliefs

and where you get them from." "Father," I said, 79
"I believe what you believed when you ran
to overtake younger feet at Christ's tomb,

and knew that he had risen from the dead.   82
I believe in one eternal God who,
unmoved, moves all by His loving desire.

My proofs are in philosophy, moral   85
and natural, and in the deeds and words
of Moses and the prophets and the psalms

and you, after the Pentecostal fire   88
gave you the gift of tongues. And I believe
in the Three Eternal Persons who are

One Being, threefold, reconciling both   91
He is and *They are*, a Divinity
stamped in me often by the Gospel text,

I believe this spark in me is growing   94
to a star that will shine in Paradise."
Increasing brightness signified his glee.

Excellent teachers will at times embrace   97
students who show they learned their lesson well.
Spun thrice round me that apostolic light

to show again that what I said was right.   100

25: Saint James and John

1   I have grown thin through working years upon
this sacred song both Heaven and earth require.
Perhaps it may persuade my enemies

4   who drove me from the town where I was born,
a lamb among ferocious wolves, to change
their minds, invite me back with sharper horn,

7   thicker fleece, stronger bleat, to be crowned as
Italy's Laureate within the Kirk
where I was christened of this faith that had

10 Saint Peter welcome me to Paradise.
Here he thrice circled around me before
from out that part of the sphere wherein shine

13 our Lord's apostles, a new glory came.
"See the noble James," my guide now murmured,
"Brother of Saint John and martyred in Spain

16 where pilgrims worship at his shrine." I saw
Peter and James converse, rotating round
each other like mating doves, then both gazed

19 so steadily at me, I had to cringe
and look away. Laughing, Beatrice said,
"O famous poet! Only living soul

chosen to see the court of Paradise   22
and show the world its generosity!
To make good hope resound about this height

you must meet Peter, James and John, the three   25
to whom their Master showed the greatest light."
"Lift up your head! take comfort!" declared James,

the second glory, adding, "At this height   28
everyone will be ripened by our rays."
So I raised my eyes to those whose greatness

previously held them down, then James said,   31
"God's grace has brought you to meet face to face
those of His inner cabinet, that you

may strengthen in yourself and others hope   34
that lets love flourish on the earth below.
So first of all let me examine you.

Say what hope is, how grows in you, and whence   37
hope came." She who had winged me here replied,
"Our Kirk has nobody more full of hope

than this our Sun has chosen for His Grace.   40
Yes, he may enter new Jerusalem
from out the land of bondage into which

he must return. You ask for two more facts,   43
not because you don't know his answers, but
to show how much you value hopeful speech.

He will answer for himself easily,   46
not boasting, for God's Grace will be his help."
Like student keen to see his master smile,

49 "Hope," said I, "is sure expectation of
glory to come, made by God's Grace in souls
purged fully of old sins. This light reached me

52 from many stars, but first King David's psalm
inspired the surest hope. He sang *Let them
hope in Me who know My name*. I who was

55 baptised knew it well. To David's stream
of hope your own Epistle added more, so
satisfied, I now try to satisfy

58 others with what I know." In that fire's heart
flashes like lightning were repeated while
I spoke, then it breathed this: "The love of hope

61 still burns in me and always will so please,
say more what hope now promises to you."
Said I, "Old and new scriptures tell the goal

64 God provides for his friends. They point me here.
Isaiah says, *All reaching their own land
are clothed, body and soul, in double robes*.

67 Your brother John proclaims the robes are white.
The promised land is here." When I said this
I heard above, "Hope is in all of you."

70 All choirs in Paradise repeated that,
and a great star among them shone as bright
as any in the zodiac. As at

73 wedding feasts a happy maiden dances,
not just for fun, but honouring the bride,
I saw this new splendour join the two flames'

dance to the anthem that proclaimed their love.   76
Said Beatrice, "See John, who Christ loved most
of His disciples and when crucified,

begged him to care for His mother Mary."   79
As after eclipse folk have been blinded
by suddenly the sun striking their eyes,

I realised my eyes had lost their sight.   82
"Why blind yourself to see what is not here?"
said John. "My earthly body will stay there

till our number equals the full sum God   85
requires. My brothers in this company
are only lights allowed to come so high.

Take this report back to your world." At this 88
the flaming sphere fell silent, with the sound
of the saints' sweetly mingled breath, just as

at a whistle's sound, oarsmen stop rowing   91
to avoid danger or fatigue. O, how
troubled I was not to see Beatrice,

though she was by my side in Paradise!   94

26: Saint John

1 While dreading blindness from the splendid flame
   that sealed my eyes, I heard these words breathed out:
   "You will not be sightless long. Your Lady

4 will mend your vision soon, and until then
   attend my words. Tell me all your desires."
   Said I, "Sight may return as soon or late

7 as she requires. My eyes were doors open
   to her. She entered them, starting the fires
   that burn within me still. She is the court,

10 Alpha and Omega, all the love that
   the Old and New Testaments mean to me."
   He said, "Make that point clearer. Your target,

13 say what that is. What goal attracts your bow?"
   Said I, "The logic of philosophy
   plus the Authority maintained here, prove

16 Love stamps its form on all that it creates;
   That Great Good is the essence of us all.
   Nothing exists outside it but stray rays

19 seeking their souls, as Aristotle knows,
   Plato demonstrates. Christians also know
   Eternity loves the products of time.

The Bible author told Moses this, said   22
I will make all my goodness pass before
your eyes, Exodus, Chapter 33.

You wrote that too, starting your Gospel with,   25
In the beginning was the Word! More than
any other words, these announce the Love

that made the universe is meant for all."   28
Said John, "Human reason and both Scriptures
all harmonise for you in Beatrice,

your strongest love that looks to God above.   31
Tell me, what other cords tie you to Him?
Name all the teeth with which love's biting you."

John the Evangelist, eagle of Christ,   34
thus made his purpose plain to me. I saw
where he was directing my confession.

I began again. "All that bites my heart   37
turns it Godward. His charity is seen
in the death he bore that everyone

might live and enjoy His works forever.   40
I hope for that as all believers do.
Love of lesser things, Beatrice expels.

Only Heaven's justice remains," said I.   43
As soon as I fell silent through the air
of Paradise resounded a sweet song

in which my Lady joined with all the rest: 46
"Holy, holy, holy." When piercing light
breaks through sleep, driving clouds of night away,

49 wakened, we may recoil from what at first
we see, but need some time to recognise.
Beatrice by her brightness now dispersed

52 my darkness. I saw better than before
and gazed amazed at a fourth brilliance
shining at our side. My Lady explained,

55 "This radiance now shows the love he feels
for being first man made to be like God."
As saplings bend before a gust of wind

58 then spring up straight again by their own force
so did I while she spoke, first bowing low
in wonder, then erect, burning to say:

61 "You only fruit created wholly ripe!
O ancient father of all folk who are
your grandsons or daughters! Please tell me what

64 you know I want to know. I will not now
delay your answer with another word."
Sparkles within that splendour made me sure

67 he answered gladly as he said, "I see
your mind can truly mirror anything
existing less than God. You're keen to know

70 how long we lived in earthly paradise –
and Hell before raised here – and the whole cause
of the Almighty's wrath – and the speech we used.

73 My son, know that Eve and me were expelled
not for only eating that fruit, but for
our pride in knowing more than people should.

In Limbo we longed to be here for four   76
thousand, three hundred and two years before
your Lady went there five days ago to

summon Virgil for your aid. When on earth   79
I saw the sun go round the zodiac
nine hundred and thirty times. Long before

Nimrod's folk built what they could not complete,   82
the tongue I spoke had vanished totally.
No work of human reason lasts more than

a few centuries. Your minds need Heaven   85
to renew them when some generations
start again. Nature forces speech on men

but lets them please themselves how it will go.   88
Before I went to Hell the Supreme Good
that gives me now such joy I then called *El*.

Later He was as suitably named *Jah*.   91
Mortal doings are much like leaves on trees.
One goes, another comes. On that mountain

rising highest from the sea we lived pure   94
then guilty from my first day's noontime bright
until the sixth day when the sun declined

leaving we two feeling ashamed at night."   97

27: To the Empyrean

1   *Glory to Father, Son and Holy Ghost!*
     The full choir of the host of Heaven sang
     that hymn so sweetly, I grew drunk on it.

4   Through ears and eyesight rapture entered me.
     I seemed to see a smiling universe
     of joy unspeakable. With love and peace

7   the four bright torches flamed before my eyes,
     the first one growing brighter till it seemed
     like Jupiter's eagle, feathered with stars

10   like those of Mars with rubies at their hearts.
     The choir fell silent as the eagle spoke.
     "Don't wonder at me changing. You will see

13   more changes soon. He who in Rome usurps
     my place, *my* place, *my* place has emptied it
     in the eyes of the Son of God! This pope

16   has made my tomb a pit of blood and shit.
     Lucifer was expelled from here but now
     triumphs below." Then Heaven was suffused

19   with angry colours that we see in clouds
     that face the rising and the setting sun.
     My Lady's colour changed like a chaste girl's

hearing news of a sister's shame. I think   22
this Heavenly eclipse the same as seen
when Jesus, crucified, gave up the Ghost.

His words continued in a voice as changed   25
as his appearance was: "The Bride of Christ –
our Holy Kirk – was not fed by my blood

nor that of many martyred saints, to gain   28
gold for the Vatican. Popes Sixtus,
Pius, Callixtus, Urban wept and bled

to reach this happy sphere. They did not use   31
my image on a battle flag in wars
with Christian foes, nor on sealed documents

telling the lie that purchasers will not   34
be damned to Hell. No wonder I've turned red!
From here I see in every Christian flock

a hungry wolf wearing a shepherd's frock!   37
O God defending us, do you still sleep?
The French popes are prepared to drink our blood!

O lovely Origin, what foulness now   40
engulfs our Kirk? But it will not end thus.
When she was prone, Scipio saved Rome

to be the glory of the world. Just so   43
swift Providence will bring salvation soon.
So you, my son, have now this mighty task.

Return to earth and tell what you have learned.   46
Say it out loud. Don't hide what I do not.
That is the reason you're permitted here."

49 In winter when the sun's in Capricorn
   the flakes of frozen vapour fall to earth.
   The coloured forms I saw now paled to white,

52 snowed upward out of sight. I was staring
   after them when Beatrice said, "And now
   look down to see how far we have revolved."

55 I did, saw it was noon, viewed the full globe
   in a broad arc from Spain to Asia –
   from the mad ocean route Ulysses took

58 to seas Europa swam astride a bull.
   I could have seen more of earth's threshing floor
   had not the sun below my feet been some

61 degrees ahead. But now I yearned to look
   into the eyes of Beatrice, for she
   to me was the full sum of Paradise.

64 If art or nature ever made a bait
   to catch the eye and occupy the mind,
   I never saw any whose charms, combined,

67 could move me from divine delight I found
   in my sweet darling's face. Her glance gave strength
   to soar to an even higher Heaven,

70 a swifter zone and yet so uniform
   I cannot say just where we entered in.
   She knew how love of knowledge masters me,

73 so said, with an ecstatic smile from which
   God's meaning seemed to glow, the following:
   "The stable order of the universe

turns round the earth, that one unmoving place,   76
but here is generated time and space.
Such is the mind of God whose love and light

creates all. Only the All-Containing   79
comprehends how everything derives
its motions from this sphere whose centre is

everywhere and boundaries nowhere.   82
Here none can see those roots whose branches sprout
the leaves and blooms and fruits of other spheres.

O why has such abominable greed   85
corrupted all who've grown from Adam's seed?
Innocent love is found in tiny bairns,

yet perishes before their cheeks grow hair.   88

28: The Angelic Sphere

1 As she who had imparadised my soul
   described the wretched human state below
   I gazed into her eyes. They snared me. She

4 Was everything I loved and wished to know.
   When looking in a mirror, if we see
   a sudden brightness shine behind our head

7 we turn to find out why. I now did that
   and saw a point of radiance so bright
   I had to close my eyes or lose my sight

10 till I received the strength to look. Sometimes
   the sun appearing through the mist will cast
   a halo round itself. This light had one –

13 a spinning ring of glory, rainbow-like,
   and round that ring a second ring; round that
   a third. I counted nine concentric rings.

16 The inmost, closest to Intensity
   of Light, was swiftest and their speed decreased
   with the much greater vastness of their arc,

19 and the inmost was incandescently
   brightest because (I think) nearest that Point,
   that Scintilla, that Essence of all light.

My lady saw how great my excitement,   22
and to ease it said, "From that one Point hangs
all the Heavens of Paradise and all

of nature's law. Of course the closest ring   25
is driven fastest by the burning love
that impels the rest." Said I, "Of course, and

if the universe showed the arrangement   28
of these wheels I would be satisfied, but
in the sensual world where I was born,

the spheres are more divine the further from   31
the earth, which is the jail of Lucifer.
If I am here to learn all good men can,

even in this angelic sphere of which   34
the only boundaries are light and love,
I must be taught why the earthly order

is reversed." Said she, "That your fingers   37
cannot untie this knot is no surprise,
since hardly anybody tries. Since your

searching mind demands satisfaction, test   40
it on this. The size of spheres depends on
how much of virtue occupies their parts.

More excellence creates more blessedness;   43
more blessedness makes bigger bodies when
the parts are perfect too; therefore this zone

which gives all motion to the universe   46
holds most people who both love and know.
If you assess the virtue, not the look

49 of spirits who appear to you as spheres
   the correspondence of intelligence
   and magnitude will become obvious."

52 As north-east gales clear our Italian skies
   sweeping the clouds away and Heaven smiles
   in all the beauty of its pageantry,

55 my Lady's answer did the same for me –
   I saw the truth as plain as Heaven's stars.
   She fell silent and each Heavenly light

58 in those nine zones, like iron filings flung
   into flames, sparkled brighter and rang out
   a hymn of praise to the Fixed Point that held

61 each in their place upon a spinning ring,
   a hymn as glad as it will always be.
   Beatrice, seeing my new confidence,

64 said, "The inmost circles to the Point hold
   the cherubim, seraphim and also
   the Thrones of Sacred Aspect who complete

67 the first trio. All angels take delight
   to the extent that their sight penetrates
   the truth in which all intellects find rest.

70 From this it can be seen that blessedness
   depends on acts of vision, not of love
   which follows it. Depth of vision gives measure

73 of merit got by God's Grace and right will,
   and thus we graduate from step to step.
   The second trio in this flowering,

this endless spring no autumn will destroy,   76
sing their hosannas in a threefold choir:
of the dominions and virtues and powers.

Last trio in this mighty festival –   79
principalities, archangels, angels
who spend eternity at play. All these

by gazing up to God prevail below,   82
in ranks that Dionysius described.
Pope Gregory disagreed with him till

opening his eyes in Heaven, he laughed   85
to see how wrong he'd been. Where that pure saint
mistook the Heavenly Host, no wonder

at first you found their discipline obscure."   88

29: Of the Angels

1   The long horizon of the gloaming sky
    linked the declining sun in the far west
    with the far east and the ascending moon.

4   It held them balanced till the moon climbed up,
    the sun dropped down to their next hemisphere.
    In that soft interval my Lady smiled

7   quietly, happily, at the fixed Point
    whose rays had lately almost hurt my sight.
    "I will not ask," said she, "I'll say instead

10 the words you want to hear, reading them from
    this Point at which time–space, where–when unite
    in the eternal, infinite *I AM*

13 Whose love made everything, archangels
    first. Only God's Spirit can say how they
    flashed into being, movers of the spheres

16 of which, with later potencies, they were
    a very grand and necessary part.
    Jerome believed long ages passed between

19 their coming and the first week of the world
    forgetting that in Genesis we read
    God's Spirit did not rest or sleep but *moved*

upon the waters of the deep before   22
creating light. Angels could not be left
without the ecstasy of serving Him,

so now your wish to know where, when and why   25
they were created should be satisfied.
Know also hardly twenty seconds passed

before rebels among them, mad with pride,   28
declared they would not serve, and so were flung
down to the lowest element, the earth,

convulsing, warping it into the pit,   31
jailing the foul monstrosities you saw
when Virgil led you through. The rest remain

delighting in their art, for it maintains   34
the universal harmony they love,
God's Grace expanding their intelligence

to fit the vastness of their mighty task.   37
Don't doubt the merit of receiving Grace
in strengthening a sure and steadfast will.

If you have fully understood these words,   40
ponder the spirits gathered in this place.
Too many Doctors of Divinity

preach about angels' mind and memory,   43
confusing hearers with obscurity.
To banish pointless ambiguity

I will say more. The angels live in sight   46
of God from whom nothing is hid. Between
Himself and they no interruption stood.

49 So they need no impressions of the past.
Preachers who speak of what they do not know
dream while awake. If they believe their words

52 yet still they are to blame. Some preachers spout
doctrines to show how very wise they are,
and this provokes less anger here than their

55 neglect of what Christ said and did. Just think
of how much blood was shed by humble folk
whose simple speech was first to spread the news

58 that Christ had risen from the dead. Today
one preacher says that when He died the moon
eclipsed the sun, a second foolishly

61 explains the miracle another way.
Shepherds who feed their sheep with words like these
are bloating them with wind. Disciples learned

64 from Christ a Gospel, kindling from their lips
Faith, Hope and Love, which was their shield and spear.
Sermons are now so stuffed with taunts and jokes

67 that if they raise a laugh the preacher's cowl
inflates and all are pleased, but Satan builds
his nests in hoods like these. If folk could see

70 the falsehood of the pardons they receive
they'd fling them down like counterfeited coin.
I have digressed enough, so turn my eyes

73 back to your interest in Heaven's hosts.
The number of the angels can't be told
in human speech. The visionary Book

of Daniel mentions thousands of them,   76
and also tens of thousands, but nothing
more definite because the Primal Light,

illuminating all, reflects each one   79
in ways as multiple as splendours poured
upon them. Because affection flows most

to what viewers conceive, Love's sweetness glows 82
differently in each, some more, some less,
making a myriad reflections of

the pure unchanging rose of whitest white."   85

30: The Empyrean

1   The sun behind the world's vast curvature
    cast its steep cone of shadow to the height
    where constellations gleamed throughout the night

4   until a faint dawn, shining in the east
    increased, tilted the shadow to the west.
    Sky paled. The stars became invisible,

7   even the Morning Star among the rest.
    The light to which I soared with Beatrice
    was infinitely brighter than the sun:

10 a radiance that held the universe,
    so dazzling that, apart from Beatrice,
    I could not see a thing. If all I've said

13 in praise of her before was harmonised
    in a great anthem of triumphant praise
    it could not hint at her new loveliness.

16 I am like one too blinded by sun's rays
    to recollect its colour and its shape.
    From the first day I saw her as a child

19 her beauty made my verses beautiful.
    Soon I must cease from making songs to her –
    all artists' inspirations have an end.

She would go on to finer fanfares than   22
my lips can blow. She still spoke as a guide
giving good words to a departing friend.

"We have arisen high above the spheres   25
of Heaven seen from earth – here all is bright
with purest love and intellect: goodness

beatified with absolute delight.   28
When your eyesight is strengthened once again
you will find in high paradise both ranks:

redeemed mankind with angels by their side."   31
Suddenly I was shrouded yet once more
by blinding glares of mist and could not see

until she said, "Love ruling Paradise   34
welcomes new souls like this, for it prepares
each candle for a better flame." At this

I felt my mind enlarged beyond itself.   37
My vision knew nothing would baffle it.
I saw a river of splendid light flow

between banks of marvellous Spring flowers.   40
From that bright stream living sparks leapt into
the blossoms, like rubies setting themselves

in gold, then as if drunk with sweet scent, went   43
plunging back into the glorious flood
from which new living jewels sparkled out.

"Your wish to understand what you see here   46
pleases me the more it grows. To satisfy
that thirst you will now drink these waters first,"

49 my Lady said. "The flashing jewellery
exchanged between the river and the blooms
are shadows of the truths you ought to see.

52 Your mortal sight is not yet purified
enough to let in much reality."
No baby waking hungry, having slept

55 more than it should, sucks at a mother's breast
more eagerly than I flung myself down
beside the stream that would improve my eyes.

58 Hardly were the two eyelids wet when both
river and banks expanded to a space
in which the waves and blossoms were dissolved

61 till they exposed a nobler festival –
all courts of Paradise! Glory to God
for giving me the strength of sight and soul

64 to view the triumph of your kingdom there!
Now give me words to speak of what I saw!
The purest light made the Creator seen

67 by all who find their final peace in Him.
It spreads so wide, the orbit of the sun
within it is a very tiny ring.

70 There the First Mover lights the mighty width
from source and summit of its potency
down to its base. As a fine grassy hill

73 might see itself reflected in a lake
my eyes took in surrounding me over
a thousand tiers of petals, God's white rose –

the seats of blessèd souls redeemed from earth. 76
The lowest level held such piercing light
I gaped at how it reached the topmost height.

No natural perspective law worked here   79
for distance made no detail indistinct.
She who had brought me to this inmost heart,

this glowing yellow centre of God's rose   82
said, "See the blessèd white-robed multitude
in the arena of our citadel.

See how few the thrones remain unfilled.   85
Notice above one an emperor's crown.
That is for the noble Henry's soul,

summoned to rightly govern Italy   88
when she is unfit – a bad child pushing
nurse away, with Kirk undermining Crown,

pretending to support. Henry will sit   91
there before you die. God will damn that pope
with Simon Magus in the malebolge

where he will thrust his predecessor down."   94

31: Heavenly Hosts

1 The host of blessèd souls redeemed by Christ
formed round me like a rose. The angel host
made first by God to fly and see and sing

4 the glory of His goodness, visited
the many-petalled rose like bees in blooms,
their faces living flames, their wings pure gold,

7 the rest whiter than snow. Their intercourse
with the redeemed maintained ardour and peace,
nor did their flight hide anyone from view.

10 Light here permitted no obscurity.
I saw this joyful commune richly thronged
with folk of ancient times and new whose sight

13 and love combined in one continuum.
O Three-fold Light seen in a single Point
and satisfying all beholding You,

16 look down upon this storm-torn earth below!
Barbaric Goths were struck dumb when they saw
Rome and her temples. How then did I feel

19 coming from human to divine? From time
to eternity? From foul Florence to
a people just and sane? Imagine my

bewilderment. Between that and gladness   22
I was content to say nothing. Silence
seemed best. Like a pilgrim who stands refreshed

in a kirk he had vowed to reach, and means   25
to tell my folk about at home, I stared,
down and around me, seeing everywhere

faces of happiness and charity   28
lit by Another's light and their own smiles,
each movement showing graceful dignity.

One thing I had to do: see Beatrice.   31
An old man suddenly confronted me.
His robe was white, his aspect fatherly.

"O where is she?" I cried. He kindly said,   34
"Beatrice sent me here. Direct your eyes
up to the highest tier. Count three rings down.

See her upon the throne she so deserves."   37
I looked, and saw that now she wore a crown
made from Eternal Light's reflected rays.

Distance between my eyes and Beatrice   40
was greater from the sky where thunder rolls
to the sea's deepest floor. I did not care.

Her image was not dimmed by things between.   43
I prayed, "O Lady who restored my hope,
walking through Hell to save my soul, all I

have learned is due your virtue and your grace.   46
Let me keep the goodness you made in me
till death sets free a soul that, with God's help,

49 still pleases you." This was my wee prayer.
Although so far away she smiled at me,
then turned to contemplate eternal light.

52 The old saint said, "Divine love brings me here
to help end your pilgrimage. Send again
your eyes around this place, for seeing more

55 will prepare them for higher radiance.
The Queen of Heaven is here helping us.
Bernard, her faithful servant, is my name."

58 As one who comes from far away to see
the veil of our Veronica, will think
O Jesus Christ my very God, was this

61 *the face you wore on earth?* I gazed upon
the Abbot of Clairvaux, saint who founded
monasteries, so rich in charities

64 that the Mother of God in a vision
appeared to him. He read my mind and said,
"You child of grace, stop gazing at your feet!

67 To know that joyful state look higher up,
see Mary on her throne!" and so I did.
Just as the dawn horizon's eastern part

70 outshines the western where the sun goes down
I felt as if my eyes climbed up from out
a valley to a mountaintop at dawn.

73 On the highest verge of the rose I saw
a brilliant zone of light, though on each side
no soul was less distinct, and in that zone

a thousand angels played with outspread wings.   76
Smiling upon their sport and songs was She
whose beauty gives delight to all the saints.

Were I as rich in words as visioning   79
I still could not try hinting at the joy
filling me at this sight. When Bernard saw

the vision warming him now shone on me,   82
we exchanged a smile before he, turning,
looked back devotedly on Her he loved.

We stood together sharing that delight.   85

32: The Rose's Plan

1 Gazing upon the source of his delight
my co-adorer kindly lectured me
beginning with these holy words: "The wounds

4 of nails and spear that Mary ointmented
and closed, derived from Eve the beautiful
who sits below her feet. You will recall

7 Eve opened them by eating of a fruit.
In the third row below sits one you know –
Beatrice; then Jewish mothers: Rachel,

10 Sarah, Rebecca, Judith, also Ruth
grandmamma of David, king and singing
sinner of the penitential psalm.

13 After the Hebrew women's seventh tier
a separation starts. On the left side
sit those who looked for Christ before his birth,

16 for they had faith in God's Old Testament.
On the right side are seats for those who know
that Christ did come, some of them empty still.

19 Now look behind. On the side opposite
equal divisions reign. Facing our Heaven's Queen
sits John the Baptist who prepared Christ's way,

suffered the wilderness and martyrdom,   22
then went to Hell before Christ set him free.
Below him see Augustine, Benedict,

Francis and others down to where we stand,   25
but split between, as on the women's side,
good Jews and Christian men, who shall remain

until both sides are filled up equally.   28
Also see that halfway down this flower
a tier encircling us has those beneath

whose merits did not win this place for them.   31
Look and listen well. Their faces, voices
tell they are souls of children who have died

before their innocence was tested by   34
fighting to conquer sin, resist Hell's snare.
I see a doubt in you, striking you dumb.

Let me untie the knot that binds your tongue.   37
Chance accidents in Paradise, like thirst,
hunger and suffering, cannot exist.

All that befalls souls here is fitting them   40
surely as rings fit fingers, so accept
God's foresight and His Grace will give to all

their rightful place. Do not try to know more.   43
Look on her face whose face is most like Christ's.
Only her brightness can enlarge your mind."

From the first angels soaring in these heights   46
I now saw gladness raining down on her.
All that appeared before was not so full

49 of such wonder and love. I seemed to see
The Holy Dove descend, and hear the hymn
"Hail Mary, full of Grace", saw the wings spread,

52 heard on each side the divine court respond
tunefully to the divine voice. Each face
melodiously grew more glorious.

55 "O holy father whose great courtesy
in guiding me removes you from your throne,
which angel gazes so enchantedly

58 upon the Virgin, he appears on fire?"
I asked the saint. He answered, "He contains
all gallantry an angel can, so brought

61 Mary word she would bear the son of God.
Attend again, for I will point out more
nobilities in this most merciful

64 empire of the just. Upon either side
of our Queen sit the twin roots of this rose.
On her left is Adam, the first dad who

67 tasted the bitter fruit, causing the Fall.
All are engendered from his seed. Look right
where sits the Kirk's father and foundation,

70 whose keys give entrance to this bonny bloom;
beside him John, the prophet who foresaw
the tribulations Christ's Kirk had to face.

73 Beside the other rests the great guide who
led the ungrateful tribes through deserts where
he nourished them with manna from the skies.

But now time flies and soon your dream must end. 76
Good tailors cut a coat according to
the cloth available, so point your eyes

toward the Primal Love. Look into His   79
radiance deep as you can. In striving
to advance you may, for lack of God's Grace,

fall back. Pray hard for Grace. Salvation   82
lies in prayer. Follow my words with love.
Let nothing come between them and your heart."

He began his holy supplication.   85

33: Prayer and Answer

1 "O Virgin Mother, daughter of your son!
Lowly, yet raised higher than anyone!
Goal of all human striving, you are she

4 ennobling humanity, because He
who made mankind chose to be made by you.
The love that was rekindled in your womb

7 had warmth enough to let this Heaven bloom
in endless peace where you are now our sun
always at height of noon. To the souls here

10 you are incarnate charity, to those on earth
a well of living hope. Lady so great
that those who seek for Grace without your aid

13 may just as well try flying without wings.
Your kindness not only aids those who ask;
sometimes it anticipates our prayer.

16 Your mercy, pity, generosity
unite in all the good that people need.
This man was sent up from the depths of Hell,

19 seeing the lives of spirits, one by one,
and now he begs your kindness for the strength
to bear salvation's last enlightenment.

I never sought that vision for myself   22
yet join my plea with his to strengthen it.
I pray you, cleanse his sight of mortal stain

making his vision fit for such delight,   25
and afterwards I pray that you will keep
his heart pure – curb his human appetite.

Many more blessèd souls unite in this   28
prayer of mine, including Beatrice."
The eyes God loved and His Son reverenced

fixed on the supplicant and plainly showed   31
she loved devoted prayer, then she looked
to the fixed point of light that only she

could penetrate with undimmed eye. By now   34
I had achieved the end of all desire,
did not want another thing, but Bernard

with a smile told me to look up. I did   37
and found my sight, now purified, could see
the lofty beam which is the one true light.

And from that time I parted company   40
with memory and speech. It seemed a dream
of passion that remains when dreamer wakes

yet can't recall visions inspiring him.   43
That has become my state. Only a few
small drops of sweetness in my heart remain,

and this is how our tears are lost in rain   46
and thaws dissolve our footsteps in the snow.
O light supreme, more than conceivable

49 by mortal mind, grant mine again some part
   of what you let me see, and give my tongue
   some power to leave a gleam of glory

52 for my readers yet to come. Please give back
   a little to my memory, so that
   my poetry conveys your victory!

55 So piercing was the splendour of that ray
   I am convinced that had I looked away
   even an instant, it had blinded me,

58 but I sustained it until my gaze reached
   the central goodness. Bless abounding Grace!
   It let me dare to face infinite light

61 so long that my whole mind was lost in it.
   The scattered pages of the universe
   were in that deepness, with its substances,

64 accidents, relationships unified
   and bound by love into a single book.
   God by His light creates complexity,

67 yet sees it as one good grand simple shape.
   In writing this I feel my joy expand.
   Twenty-five hundred centuries ago

70 the first ship was launched. A single moment
   gazing at that light seemed more. I could not
   look elsewhere. The good which is the object

73 of all will was there. What exists outside
   is defective; all that exists within
   is perfectly made. Now know that my words

will tell even less of what I recall   76
than if my infant tongue still sucked a breast.
The living light remained the same, but I

began to change. My strengthened sight saw more. 79
In the profoundest clear ground of the light
appeared three circles, different colours

and same size. Two reflected each other   82
as rainbows do, the third took fire from them.
Alas, such blethering *cannot* convey

the things I noticed in Eternal Light   85
fulfilling, knowing, loving its sweet self
in that reflecting, circling Trinity!

As my eyes dwelled on it I seemed to see   88
a human form. Like the geometer
battering his brain in vain to find how

circles are squared, I tried to see or feel   91
how such a human form could live in light
eternally. The wings of my fancy

could not fly so far, until in a flash   94
I saw desire and will: both are a pair
of finely balanced wheels kept turning by

love that revolves sun, sky and every star.   97